MW00488981

Transcending the Personality Disordered Parent

Psychological and Spiritual Tactics

Randy A. Sansone, MD

Michael W. Wiederman, PhD

The information in this book is provided for educational purposes, and not intended as a substitute for diagnosis or treatment by a professional healthcare provider. Please consider whether professional treatment may be appropriate for you.

The information pertaining to case examples in this book has been altered to disguise the identity of the individuals described. Any resemblance between individuals described in this book and actual individuals, alive or dead, is entirely coincidental.

To Lori—

Mi amor para siempre.

—Randy

To Corinne—

May I be a better father as a result of my
less-than-ideal experiences with my own.

—Michael

The gift of truth excels all other gifts.

The Buddha

Contents

Chapter 1
Personality Disordered Parents

It's well-known that parents oftentimes take credit for their children's accomplishments. It's just as well-known that children oftentimes blame their parents for the negative ways that they have turned out. Sometimes, the blame is justifiable. Sometimes, the parents are culpable and psychologically unfit. And, sometimes, these parents suffer from personality disorders. That's what this book is about—parents with significant personality dysfunction.

In this book, we examine how the children of these parents (you?) may have been affected by their personality difficulties. Most importantly, this book also advises on how you can emotionally and spiritually transcend the effects of having been raised by such a parent.

What does a personality disordered parent look like? On the surface, these parents frequently appear very normal, especially during brief periods of contact and in superficial social settings. They may seem to get along fine with others and appear to appropriately follow social rules. They may even appear successful in their relationships with colleagues and friends, who tend to interact with them only on a limited basis. However, when the personality disordered parent disengages from the rhythm of these exterior social settings and sets aside his or her carefully constructed public mask, the family is exposed to the naked reality of blatant personality dysfunction.

While others may only catch glimpses of their elusive dysfunction, personality disordered parents typically reveal themselves to their children through the unvarnished reality of day-to-day home life. Many different types of personality disorder symptoms may be present, but the overall impression of the parent is one of social immaturity. For example, common personality disorder features that emerge from these parents include self-centeredness, emotional instability, inappropriate interpersonal behaviors, and unrestrained impulsivity or poor judgment.

What's the outcome of childhood exposure to these types of compromised parents? Unfortunately, these parents may contribute to a wide range of psychological difficulties in their children, especially as these children enter into adolescence and mature into young adults. Throughout adolescence, the children of personality disordered parents may face serious interpersonal challenges, including difficulty managing emotions (particularly anger), problems developing a solid and confident self, and struggles with genuine intimacy. While these themes are frequently challenging developmental tasks for all adolescents, having a personality disordered parent intensifies these difficulties and may undermine the child's earnest attempts to grow.

In terms of transcending a childhood spent with a personality disordered parent, the process is much like a journey. However, this journey doesn't have a well-defined end-point. In other words, while it is possible to transcend a number of the negative effects of such experiences, it is impossible to go back and undo these taxing childhood traumas. It is, however, possible to not only transcend or rise above these experiences, but to actually draw upon them as a source of psychological and spiritual growth. The starting point begins with a better understanding of your parent's dysfunctions. Although the goal here is not to diagnose your parents with a psychiatric disorder, it is important to understand what character features constitute a *personality disorder*.

What is a Personality Disorder?

What do we mean by the terms *personality* and *disorder*? Clinicians often use the term "personality" to refer to the general psychological characteristics of a person. In other words, who that person "is" aside from his or her physical body. This would include the person's thoughts, feelings, attitudes, and behaviors. Still, not every thought, feeling, attitude, or behavior indicates a person's personality. Implied in the term *personality* is the notion that the important characteristics are those that are relatively consistent and enduring over time. This is in contrast to a person's momentary behavior, which may be the result of a particular situation and/or the social expectations that come along with that situation.

Disorder refers to the existence of a problem that causes the person to be dysfunctional. That is, the disorder causes problems in the person's general life functioning, and this frequently entails problems in their relationships with others. So to summarize, personality disorders are enduring or chronic thoughts, attitudes, and behaviors that negatively impact multiple aspects of an individual's life, especially that person's relationships with others.

In addition, these personality patterns or psychological characteristics deviate from what is considered appropriate or normal in the person's culture or by their healthy peers. Notice that we're not specifying what the problematic characteristics are, because these vary depending on the person. But why they constitute a personality disorder is their inflexibility, the negative outcomes that they foster, and their deviation from "the acceptable."

The emphasis on chronicity with a personality disorder implies that the person's inner thoughts and social patterns are fairly ingrained and resistant to change. In other words, these patterns are likely to continue regardless of ongoing opportunities to learn and acquire new thoughts and behaviors in various social experiences with others. Put another way, these individuals stay stuck in their personality patterns, even though such patterns continually cause problems.

Because a person's personality is basically who that person is, individuals with personality disorders are unlikely to recognize that their personalities are the problem. They have lived with their dysfunction for a long time (in some form since childhood) and usually don't objectively understand what is affecting them, their behavior, or their relationships with others. It's one thing to temporarily be in a bad mood or to have a temporary conflict in a particular relationship. But even in the presence of ongoing problems, very few people think, "Perhaps my personality is the cause of these recurrent problems in my life." It's much more likely that they will view the cause of their problems as external—namely that they are caused by other people, even if those other people are their own children.

What Causes Personality Disorders?

As with any psychiatric disorder, particularly one that causes so many problems, it's natural to ask *why*? Why do some individuals have personality disorders and other do not? Like so many answers to complex questions, there is no "one-size-fits-all" explanation. Most likely, a personality disorder arises from a complex set of conditions that are both biological and environmental in nature.

Unfortunately, these various conditions are not well understood by researchers.

Let's consider the biological side first. Biologically, we each enter the world with an innate temperament, or set of predispositions, to react to the world in particular ways. For example, some infants are more anxious than others, some are less responsive to stimulation than others, some are more easily consoled than others, and so forth. These innate predispositions are the biological soil out of which our personalities develop. This is what researchers mean when they say that personality has a substantial genetic component.

Rather than "inherited from our parents," the term *genetic* is actually much broader and means "arising from our genetic makeup." That genetic makeup is comprised of genes that we have received from each parent and each of their genetic lineages. As a result, we represent a unique combination of those genes, which may culminate in a temperament very different from either parent (or siblings). Of course, particular temperaments may be more probable if one or both parents exhibit that specific temperament (i.e., the genetic cards would be somewhat stacked in that direction).

What about the environmental side of the personality disorder equation? For the personality disordered individual, important environmental factors probably include distressing experiences with *their* parents, trauma in childhood, and the accumulation of life stressors. Let's examine each of these factors.

Dysfunctional caregivers are a distinct contributor to the development of personality disorders. Research has shown that individuals with personality dysfunction are more likely to have parents with personality disorders than people with healthy personalities. The extent to which this connection is due to genetic factors versus parenting issues remains unclear. However, we can readily imagine the various ways in which a parent's personality dysfunction could result in unhealthy parenting styles. So, negative parental influences are one of several potential "shaping" factors for personality dysfunction in offspring.

As a second factor, trauma in childhood is not uncommon and may occur through dysfunctional parenting styles. Perhaps there is complete emotional indifference towards the child and the total absence of nurturance. Perhaps there is emotional, physical, and/or sexual abuse. There may also be intrusive over-control. Understandably, these barren and/or abusive emotional landscapes make it difficult to cultivate healthy children. Trauma may also be due to outside causes, such as molestation by an outsider or severe illness.

Given the possibility of a vulnerable temperament, dysfunctional parenting, and possible childhood trauma, individuals experiencing some set of these conditions are more likely to be subjected to stress in a variety of forms. For example, having parents who make poor decisions may result in problematic living conditions such as financial instability, poor family planning, and alcohol/substance abuse. Also, having a parent whose personality is dysfunctional may leave the child vulnerable to other dysfunctional adults who are neglectful or abusive.

Research has shown that individuals who are subjected to various types of early adverse experiences are, as a result, less able to deal with life's ongoing stressors. This impairment in dealing with stress may be reinforced by subsequent biological changes resulting from the adversity itself, inherited deficits in coping, and/or inadequate mentoring by dysfunctional parents.

Is Parental Change Out of the Question?

Because personality has such a strong genetic basis and consists of the enduring psychological essence of the individual, dramatic change is probably unlikely. While it may seem that psychotherapy would be beneficial, not all personality disorders respond equally well to such treatment. Also, because people with personality disorders are unlikely to see their own personalities as the root causes of the difficulties that they are having in their lives, they are unlikely to seek psychotherapy treatment.

Could prescription medications help? Psychotropic medications such as antidepressants, antipsychotics, and anticonvulsants appear to have only a modest role in the treatment of individuals with personality disorders. At times, these medications may be prescribed to partially relieve specific symptoms such as depression, anxiety, and impulsivity. However, most research indicates that the effects of psychotropic medications on specific personality disorder symptoms are relatively modest and short-lived.

One positive influence on personality dysfunction is maturity. Research has revealed that there may be some meaningful decrease in personality disorder symptoms with aging. The downside, however, is that this observed improvement in symptoms is likely to be more evident on a behavioral level than with regard to ways of thinking and reacting to people and events. In other words, observable behavior may improve, but the attitudes and approaches to dealing with the world remain much more resistant to change. This distinction begs the question as to whether the observed improvement with age is simply due to a decrease in energy and physical ability, resulting in less acting out. And then, unfortunately, some personality disordered individuals experience recurrent symptoms over their entire lives.

Regardless of whether symptoms gradually improve through psychotherapy, psychotropic drugs, or maturity, it is important to realize that dramatic improvements in individuals with personality disorders are unrealistic. Accordingly, one important theme in this book is to relinquish the hope that your personality disordered parent will change (or should have changed). Instead, it is more feasible to change your own perceptions and reactions in order to heal from the damage caused by your parent's personality disorder.

Although each personality disordered parent is unique, there is a common set of characteristics that are frequently displayed by such parents. We will consider these separately in the next several chapters. We will then present two broad types of personality disordered parents, with a detailed case example of each. As you read these next several chapters, ask yourself which aspects of these characteristics seem to apply to your problematic parent.

Chapter 2
Social Foolers and Outright Liars

Individuals with personality disorders tend to appear relatively normal in social and work settings yet are unable to maintain healthy close relationships, particularly with family members. This key dichotomy represents the amazing paradox of individuals with personality disorders—appearing normal to the outside world but being highly dysfunctional in close relationships with others. Let's consider the two (or more) faces of parents with personality disorders.

Masters of Masquerade

Adult children of personality disordered parents often say, "If the people at work only knew what my dad was *really* like!" or, "My mother will come in here and look really normal—but she's not and you won't see it!" These Jekyll-and-Hyde features truly capture the personality disordered parent's masterful social masquerade. As a result, individuals with personality disorders are epitomized by both "normal" and "not-normal" selves, constituting an inconsistency or paradox that frequently leaves the children of such parents confused.

We might say that parents with personality disorders tend to be social *foolers*. While all of us put our best foot forward in particular situations, such as in dating relationships or work interviews, personality disordered parents do so in ways that are far removed from their baseline personality. In contrast, for healthy individuals, there is a greater consistency between the self at work and the self at home. Again, for individuals with personality disorders, this sense of consistency is oftentimes lacking.

Consider a nurse with a personality disorder. At work, she may appear attentive, caring, and emotionally available to her patients. However, conforming to the standards of appropriate behavior does not come naturally for personality disordered individuals. Presenting a façade of normalcy requires a great deal of emotional energy. As a result, these individuals cannot maintain that same level of "normal" functioning indefinitely.

Unfortunately, it's oftentimes at home with family that parents with disordered personalities "let down" their monitored façades. The personality disordered nurse who was so competent and caring at work is now at home, yelling and screaming, and consuming an excessive amount of vodka as she verbally berates her children.

The ability to socially fool others has another important implication—dating relationships. Because dating involves relatively brief periods of being on one's best behavior, the personality disordered individual may be able to successfully mask his or her underlying psychopathology for these modest spans of time. If successful in continuing to mislead dating partners over the span of the courtship, the personality disordered individual may get married. However, once the marriage is actualized, the spouse of the personality disordered individual unexpectedly begins to see the previously "hidden" personality dysfunction. The healthier spouse soon recognizes that he/she made a serious mistake in marrying this individual. This hold-it-together-until-we-get-married dynamic may explain the seemingly common commentary, "He/she really changed once we got married—he/she is a totally different person, now!"

The preceding unfortunate outcome may be explained by the combination of social fooling, in which the pathological partner was able to maintain an appropriate yet superficial social façade while in the dating relationship, as well as the presence of minimal stressors during the dating relationship. Typically, as life becomes more complex through marriage (i.e., a full-time relationship with new life demands such as mortgages, in-laws, and children), the façade of these impaired individuals quickly crumbles, intensifying the personality dysfunction underneath.

Lies, Lies, and More Lies

Factual Dishonesty

Social fooling may be just one variation of the general social dishonesty exhibited by parents with personality disorders. Such parents may use "little white lies" to explain away their behavioral inconsistencies and poor judgment. Typically, these "little white lies" are very minimal or negligible in nature, such that we may view the infraction as not even worth covering over with a lie. None-the-less, the lie shelters the truth.

For example, one patient recalled an incident in which her personality disordered mother was applying for a low-level job in a nursing home—one that did not require a college degree. However, the mother indicated on the job application that she had completed two years of college at the University of Maryland. When the patient saw the application form, she understandably expressed her surprise. "Mom, I didn't know that you went to the University of Maryland for two years!" Her mother replied, "I didn't, but they'll never know."

In another instance, a personality disordered mother persistently cajoled her daughter into buying a bigger home—one that would befit the young professional that her daughter had become. After the patient purchased the more expensive home, the balloon-interest mortgage rate proved to be a considerable financial strain. In response to the patient's stress, the mother berated her daughter, "Why did you need to get a bigger house in the first place?" When the daughter confronted her mother about previously pressuring her to buy a new house, the mother blankly responded, "I *never* told you to buy a bigger house!" The daughter was justifiably dumb-founded.

An important and unresolved issue is whether this factual dishonesty is actually conscious. In other words, is it intentional lying or extreme denial? In examining this issue, it's important to appreciate that personality disordered individuals are used to dysfunctional and maladaptive ways of processing information. Incoming data are filtered and colored by their own emotional needs. So, on the one hand, it is possible that these "little white lies" are simply the outgrowths of repeatedly spackling the inconsistencies in their world with a convenient social plaster of denial. At other times, however, the deceit is so blatant that it appears to be conscious and intentional. Perhaps it is. Unfortunately, regardless of the type of dishonesty (lie or denial), the result is the undermining of the foundation of the parent-child relationship. The parent simply cannot be trusted.

Emotional Dishonesty

In addition to commonplace "little white lies," personality disordered parents are oftentimes *emotionally* dishonest, as well. This subtle form of dishonesty commonly manifests in two forms—(1) expressing only the negative and (2) refusing to be vulnerable. Let's examine these two issues a bit closer.

First, personality disordered individuals appear incapable of expressing a broad and sincere range of emotions. Oftentimes, this observation appears as the tendency to under-express positive emotions and over-express negative ones. As an example of this form of emotional dishonesty, one patient recalled how her mother gave her confusing messages all of her life. When the mother said she was happy, such as when the patient got accepted to a college in another state, tears of sadness simultaneously streamed down her face. "Most of the time, I really don't know *what* she is trying to communicate to me, but it always seems negative!" the patient reported in therapy.

In addition to unbalanced emotional expression with a disproportionate amount of the negative, emotional dishonesty may also emerge in an unwillingness to be truly vulnerable in a relationship with another person. This is likely to be a protective mechanism from a challenging childhood. "Don't be vulnerable. Never let them see you cry. Don't let them get to you." Unfortunately, this aversion to vulnerability means it is highly unlikely that the personality disordered parent will admit to wrong-doing or apologize. Such personal vulnerability or weakness can never be allowed. Because of this faulty belief, these individuals can never truly acknowledge their own mistakes or shortcomings. It's simply never their fault.

These features—"little white lies," the inability to effectively communicate deeper positive emotions, and the unwillingness to allow for vulnerability—lead to the overall impression that individuals with personality disorders are incapable of genuine honesty. This may explain why, at the outset, healthier individuals tend to steer clear of people with personality disorders. Healthier individuals tire of what they see as the one-sided "games" and pretenses of these people, and move on to partners who are able to participate in an emotionally mature relationship founded on candor and honesty. Unfortunately, children growing up with a personality disordered parent rarely have that luxury.

Ask Yourself . . .

Do you recall feeling like people outside your family really did not know what your parent was like?

Do you recall instances in which your parent lied to different people, perhaps about relatively small things or when it was not really necessary to lie?

Do you recall feeling like your parent maintained an emotional wall, perhaps by being consistently negative or critical?

How often do you recall your parent displaying genuinely positive emotions, including vulnerability and tenderness?

Sansone & Wiederman

Chapter 3
Reacting, Not Responding

A characteristic of personality disordered parents that is difficult to miss is their overly intense emotional displays. These performances of unbridled emotion are typically preceded by minor incidents and seem excessive compared to what most people would consider a socially acceptable response to those circumstances. Family may describe the personality disordered member as "overly sensitive," "too emotional," or "hot headed."

In contrast to their more modulated behaviors at work or around friends, the personality disordered parent at home tends to emotionally *react* rather than *respond*. Responding involves an appropriate level of behavior that corresponds to the situation, and frequently entails controlling one's initial feelings. Reacting involves an inappropriately high level of emotionality that is greater than the situation warrants, perhaps because the situation is simply the match for igniting a fuse to a deeper well of unresolved emotional turmoil.

This reactivity is readily evident in day-to-day life. When the home environment is calm and peaceful, without any distractions or inconveniences, the personality disordered individual may function in a somewhat normal fashion. However, when the home environment becomes demanding, chaotic, or challenging (e.g., paying bills, disciplining children, taking a sick pet to the veterinarian), the regulated behaviors of the personality disordered parent begin to quickly erode. The result? Intense and inappropriate emotional over-reacting.

As an example of inappropriate emotional reactivity, a patient described a very turbulent relationship between his father and older brother. The older brother constantly challenged parental limits, and as he did so, the limits set by the father became more stringent and unreasonable. During one incident, when the clock struck 11:00 pm and the son wasn't home as required by his curfew, the father grabbed his loaded shot gun and waited in the family room for his son's arrival. When the son returned home at 1:00 am, only verbal jabs were exchanged that night, but this dramatic (and potentially dangerous) episode emotionally traumatized the family for days.

In an attempt to curb these emotional meltdowns, the personality disordered individual may demand an unrealistically conflict-free home environment. In response, a fearful spouse may tentatively accommodate such a need by attempting to create an artificial home environment that is free of any problems, which makes sense. By eliminating any semblance of problems in the home, the personality disordered partner is far less likely to emotionally combust. However, this maneuver is precarious. The personality disordered parent becomes accustomed to these periods of unrealistic calm in the home and expects this to be the norm. Realistically, however, families aren't consistently calm. There are unending disturbances in the moment-to-moment rhythms of family life. As a result of this maneuver, the healthier spouse and children ultimately dance on pins and needles, hoping for the best and waiting for the inevitable—a disruption, a problem, a conflict.

Patterns of volatility may become so predictable that the healthier spouse actually anticipates and plans around them. For example,

"Let's get things all picked up—Daddy's coming home soon and we don't want to upset him!"

Likewise, in response to household "crises," the personality disordered parent may reflexively blame the spouse for not maintaining the Nirvana that he or she expected ("It's *your* fault that the kid's sick, again!"). After all, the partner unconsciously agreed to perform this accommodating function and has now failed.

Once the pattern is recognizable, children oftentimes develop a keen sense of emotional forecasting with regard to what to expect from their personality disordered parent on a given day or following a specific event. "It's Friday night—she'll start drinking right after dinner, yell a lot, and the drama will finally end around 9:00 pm, when she passes out." One patient recalled how her intoxicated step-parent would repeatedly return home from a night of drinking, rouse the three children from their beds, order them into a queue, and then verbally berate them, one by one. This nightmarish drama persisted for years. It was as predictable as the rising and setting sun.

Emotional reacting rather than responding doesn't involve just emotional outbursts. Personality disordered parents are frequently impulsive, and end up making poor judgments and decisions. Examples include excessive drinking, drug use, and cigarette smoking; promiscuity and infidelity; eating disorders such as binge-eating and obesity; and difficulty with managing money such as gambling and overspending with credit cards. In extreme cases, there may be physical violence and/or suicide attempts.

In cases of alcohol and/or substance misuse, the children of parents with personality disorders may simplistically label their dysfunctional parent as an alcoholic or drug addict. Logically and understandably, the adult child attempts to explain away the parent's dysfunctional behavior in terms of addiction. However, while alcoholism and addictions truly are significant problems because of the effects of intoxication and long-term brain effects, these substances also tend to magnify or intensify personality pathology (i.e., things get worse because the drugs or alcohol remove inhibitions on dysfunctional tendencies).

From a developmental perspective, it is likely that the impulsivity and poor judgment observed in substance-using individuals are actually symptoms of underlying psychological patterns that developed in childhood and now make up the individual's personality disorder. Once the personality disorder is established, impulse problems such as alcohol or drug abuse become established, which then fuel and exacerbate the underlying personality dysfunction. In these circumstances, the resulting social dysfunction and offensive behaviors of the user are rarely *just* the result of alcoholism or drugs; personality dysfunction is often the culprit as well.

Last, reacting rather than responding may be displayed through rigid automatic responses in relationships. People with healthy personalities are able to adapt and customize their behavior to the relationships they have with different people and in different circumstances, and to learn from experiences with other people. In contrast, parents with personality disorders tend to hold fixed and unyielding styles of misperceiving and responding to others, regardless of who they are (e.g., the neighbor or the boss). These dysfunctional patterns are the result of their rigid and inflexible internal wiring, and tend to result in repetitive destructive behaviors across relationships.

A common example of destructive recurrent behavior is the repetition of verbal phrases or clichés by the personality disordered parent in interactions with others. Personality disordered individuals frequently repeat themselves with well-worn expressions. Examples include, "It's always your fault!," "Everyone *always* disappoints me," and, "You've *hurt* me for the last time." Clichés such as these become quite familiar to the children of parents with personality disorders. One patient reported that she grew up with, and still hears, the tiresome commentary from her mother, "I know that you love your father more than me; I know that you don't love me." Another reported that, after insisting on getting his way, the patient's father would always inaccurately conclude, "See, I'm not hard to get along with." Wearisome, annoying, and never varying, these verbal clichés exemplify the fixed dysfunctional patterns that characterize personality disordered parents and serve to push their children away.

Ask Yourself . . .

While you were growing up, was your parent overly emotional or prone to outbursts?

In your family, did it seem that members had to be careful in their behavior in hopes of keeping the problematic parent from getting upset?

Looking back now, as an adult, did your parent exhibit problems controlling impulses or show poor judgment, thereby making bad decisions?

Do you recall predictable patterns in which parental outbursts tended to occur? Was there a typical scenario or sequence?

Did your parent express predictable verbal phrases when he or she was upset?

Chapter 4
It's All About Me, Me, Me

The personality disordered parent frequently comes across as extremely self-centered. It seems like the parent is sending out a universal broadcast that says, "It's truly all about me." From this basic theme, parental self-absorption takes many shapes and forms. For example, the personality disordered person may continually divert conversations to focus on him- or herself. "No matter what we talk about, my mother always shifts the conversation back to herself. If I say I have back pain, she says *she* has back pain. If I have a bad day, she's had a bad day. And of course it's always worse than mine."

As another example, this "me-me-me" theme may be expressed through a preoccupation with personal belongings. Personality disordered individuals may believe that their belongings (e.g., clothes, cars, houses, jewelry), simply by association, are of superior value or importance. For example, one patient indicated that her personality disordered mother lived in clutter and squalor. When the family attempted to remove the rubbish, the mother, who was quite aged, aggressively threatened the offenders. Why? Because the mother believed that her belongings were genuine antiques and of immeasurable value. When questioned about the value of these belongings, the patient heartily laughed and responded, "It's just junk."

As for a more bizarre example of self-absorption, one patient disclosed that she and her personality disordered mother got into a fight on the telephone because the mother was tearfully lamenting the loss of her dog, Macky. Initially, it was unclear how this sentiment of loss developed into a mother/daughter conflict. Then the patient indicated that her mother *never had a dog*. On the contrary, it was the *patient* who had owned a dog named Macky, who had passed away. Apparently, the personality disordered mother was so self-absorbed that she had literally high-jacked a memory that belonged to her daughter. And why? Seemingly to narcissistically elicit attention and sympathy from others.

One of the true tragedies of this intense level of self-absorption is that the personality disordered parent is rarely aware of, and therefore unable to acknowledge, appreciate, or respond to the genuine feelings and emotions of others. Their emotional radars are seemingly aimed in one direction—towards themselves. This lack of empathy and the inability to emotionally resonate with others is frequently the cause of ongoing relationship discord.

As an example, one patient described her mother's tedious demands for time and attention. The patient's mother repeatedly pressured her to meet for breakfast at a local restaurant every day before the patient went to work. When the patient was too busy and unable to free up the time to meet for breakfast, her mother became predictably whiny and antagonistic. "Well, I guess there are more important things in your life than time with me."

As another example, a patient described her mother's ongoing pattern of asking her to make trips to the store to buy clothes and household items, including furniture and a television. Invariably, upon returning to the parent's house with the requested purchases, the mother deemed each to be wrong for one reason or another, and every item was subsequently returned to the store. After years of this manipulative behavior, the patient recognized the dysfunctional pattern and discussed it with her father. Without hesitation, he explained that his wife's continual dissatisfaction with everything was the reason why he never bought a house but always rented one—she would never be pleased with *any* house. Likewise, the mother was *never* pleased with either her daughter or her husband.

The characteristic lack of empathy that is observed in personality disordered parents naturally causes serious difficulties in the raising of children. Children learn to emotionally trust themselves and value themselves through parents who mirror or reflect back their emotional experiences and appropriately affirm them. "Mommy, I fell and hurt myself," is supposed to elicit a response such as, "I saw what happened, honey! You *did* fall—are you okay? How's my little sweet pea?" Instead, personality disordered parents rarely value or empathize with anyone but themselves. Therefore, they don't think about or respond to the emotional needs of others, including their children. The ongoing absence of this validating mirroring behavior by the dysfunctional parent tends to result in a child who lacks confidence in his or her own feelings and perceptions. In addition, due to a lack of healthy parental affirmation, these children typically develop into adults who suffer from insecurity based on a poor self-concept and low self-esteem.

As the failure in parental empathy continues, the child may begin to suppress his/her own needs in service of the parent's narcissistic needs, which are seen as more important. This may result in the child having lifelong difficulties openly acknowledging and negotiating their own personal needs in relationships with others. This particular deficit is a genuine liability for the adult child and may culminate in numerous unfulfilling relationships.

Because of the self-centered nature of the personality disordered parent, the child tends to be perceived as a burden—initially by the parent, and then by the child. How does the child come to this conclusion? Easily. Most of the personal needs of the child are unfairly perceived by the personality disordered parent as inconvenient or unnecessary. "Why do you need that?" The conclusion by the child? "I'm not that important."

One patient recalled that, while growing up, her mother literally placed price tags on everything that she bought for her daughter. As a result, clothes, toiletries, and all other necessities were imbued with the feeling, "You owe me," or "Look at what you cost me."

Another patient sadly reminisced that, regardless of the request, whether for lunch money, a new pair of shoes to replace worn-out ones, or an extra serving at dinner, the personality disordered father consistently replied, "You don't need that, you don't need that, you don't need that!" The patient and his four siblings were routinely subjected to the same offensive response, so it couldn't really be taken too personally. However, the patient clearly believed that he and his siblings were unwanted—they were considered five inconveniences to the father. Understandably, they believed themselves to be burdens and liabilities because they had needs. As a result of growing up with this type of parent, neither the patient nor any of his siblings had any children of their own. The message had been well communicated—children are an intolerable burden.

As the child grows up and recognizes the parent's personality dysfunction, the adult child oftentimes emotionally abandons the dysfunctional parent ("It's too much work to spend time with him/her!"). In response, the dysfunctional parent typically launches a blame campaign about the adult child to anyone who will listen. The blame campaign is ironically loaded with projections—characteristics of the personality disordered parent that are erroneously projected onto the adult child as characteristics of that child. "You know, he's the most self-centered bastard I know!" "She's so cold and indifferent—I don't know where she gets that from!" "All she cares about is herself! I never raised her that way!" "She only calls when she needs something." On and on, one projection after another. In the end, these projections only serve to legitimize the adult child's decision to seek emancipation from the parent.

Ask Yourself . . .

Looking back now to your childhood, did your parent seem considerably more self-centered than most other adults?

Do you recall feeling frustrated that your parent seemed unable or unwilling to see important issues from your perspective? (It's not that your parent had to agree with you, but was he or she able to empathize and understand why you felt the way you did?)

While growing up, did you feel like your parent experienced you as a burden, or only as a set of "costs"?

How often did your parent complain about the "costs" associated with being a parent?

Chapter 5
Bullies and Victims

In many individuals with personality pathology, there are the emotional themes of sadism (being a bully) and masochism (being the bullied). These roles may even oscillate within the same individual. In the sadistic position, the personality disordered parent may be demeaning, overly controlling, derogatory, debasing, and even emotionally, physically, and sexually abusive. In the masochistic position, the personality disordered parent may allow abuse from others (e.g., partner violence), engage in self-defeating behaviors (e.g., alcohol abuse, sabotaging a job), and continually gravitate towards emotionally victimizing relationships with others. In this latter masochistic position, personality disordered individuals seem to unconsciously embrace an overall lack of success in life. Although either of these emotional positions may be directed towards the child, the sadistic position is seemingly the more overtly toxic one.

Sadistic parents can engage in a number of noxious behaviors. For example, verbal abuse is commonly encountered in sadistic parents with personality disorders. Verbal abuse oftentimes takes the form of lengthy and debasing sessions in which the parent chews out the child. As an example, one patient commented that her narcissistic husband used to punish their two sons by "bitching at them for hours on end" about an infraction. As the boys sat on the edge of their beds, the father angrily berated them and criticized them for literally several hours, with intermittent yelling and screaming—only inches from their faces.

Another patient shared a sadistic verbal experience with regard to her personality disordered father, who was a dentist. He was a sermonizer, who his daughter referred to in therapy as "Dr. Lecture." This moniker was used to describe his unending passion for monotonous and lengthy discourses to anyone who would listen. No matter the issue, regardless of how mundane ("What time are you getting home?"), there was always a lengthy and entrapping response.

At its subtlest level, parental verbal abuse may be undertaken through teasing. This behavior is particularly common through reference to another family member. "Oh, Jamie has the same nose as Aunt Gwen!," or "Jared is as slow (mentally) as Uncle Bart!" In most cases, the unwanted family characteristic is unfairly assigned to the child to tease or criticize the child in a "friendly" way.

At its worst, parental verbal abuse may entail a direct attack on the personal attributes of the child. One patient commented that his father used to repetitively rant in a debasing tone, "You don't listen, you don't listen, you don't listen." When asked for an example of what might prompt this response, the patient described how he would ask his father for driving directions, yet only receive verbal directions, never written ones. As a teen driver, unfamiliar with the roads, the patient continually got lost and was habitually late. In response, the father would angrily blame his son for "not listening, not listening, not listening." The father absolutely refused to write down any directions. As the patient reached adulthood, he began to realize that the directions given by his father were invariably wrong. Rather than admit that he didn't know the correct directions, the personality disordered father apparently made up directions and then blamed his child for getting lost. In this way, the father could maintain the illusion of being knowledgeable and competent, and sadistically abuse his child at the same time.

As another example of a direct attack on a child's attributes, one patient described his experience of maltreatment from his mother. Whatever the mistake, however big or small, he was chronically impaled with a screaming screeching voice, "Danny, you're stupid, stupid, stupid! Why can't you learn? You're so stupid!" This response occurred on a regular basis for years, almost as if it were a reflexive response to any infraction. As expected, the patient believed himself to be truly incompetent and lacked self-confidence as an adult, despite his successful completion of a master's degree.

In a forlorn case of both verbal abuse and betrayal, one patient described her mother's response to her pregnancy in high school, which was the result of date rape. When disclosed by the daughter, the mother angrily sent her off for an abortion. "My mother was really pissed! She yelled and screamed, and then wouldn't talk to me for days. She threatened me to within an inch of my life not to tell anyone—after all, what would the neighbors think of my being pregnant?" The rapist was a somewhat older male in the neighborhood, with whom the mother continued to *intentionally* socialize so that "things would appear normal." The patient understandably felt betrayed by her mother, who seemed to place social appearances above her daughter's wellbeing.

In addition to various forms of verbal abuse, sadistic behaviors may include blatantly unfair and excessive physical discipline. For example, one patient was beaten on her legs and stomach with a belt by her father because she broke curfew with a girlfriend. Following the beating, the 16-year-old patient was placed in the basement of the family home for two days without food.

Another female patient was bizarrely punished by her mother for "talking back." As the 15-year-old patient ran up the stairs to escape her out-of-control mother (who was intoxicated), the personality disordered mother tackled her and shoveled a handful of Vick's Vapo-Rub™ into her mouth as punishment.

A male patient shared his painful experience of piano practice with his father. His father, an accomplished musician, would guide the teaching sessions with a belt in hand, striking the belt against the piano bench like a metronome. Each and every technical mistake by the child was threatened with corporeal punishment by the father.

Finally, one patient indicated that his father used to beat him on the head with a belt buckle to help him control his impulsive behavior, which was attributed to attention deficit hyperactivity disorder. The patient misinterpreted his father's abusive behavior and clarified that, "My dad was really trying to help me control myself."

While perhaps not intended as such, all of the preceding behaviors are essentially sadistic and represent bullying (the strong—in this case, the personality disordered parent—unfairly taking advantage of the weak). From the parent's perspective, he or she is likely doing what a good parent needs to do to raise "good" children. In reality, the personality disordered parent is repeating and acting out the same negative verbiage and abusive behaviors that he or she was exposed to as a child. These toxic patterns may continue for generations, from parent to child, until a given individual experiences sufficient personal insight to disrupt the cycle.

Ask Yourself . . .

In particular relationships with other adults, did your parent seem to take on either a victim or martyr role?

Do you recall instances in which you were disciplined in ways that were harsher, or more excessive, than the ways other kids your age were disciplined?

How often did your parent "tease" you or put you down in ways that were hurtful and belittling?

Looking back now, as an adult, did your parent engage in behaviors that you would consider verbally or physically abusive?

Chapter 6
Adding Children

Fortunately, infants and very young children place relatively low emotional demands on parents. Yes, taking care of them can be stressful for the parent, but the child's needs are predominantly physical during those very early years of life. As a result, the emotional complications that may arise in the parent/child relationship seem to be more evident as the child matures. This is not to say that poor emotional management during infancy and early childhood is without cost, but that cost may not fully show itself until later childhood — particularly adolescence.

Interestingly, the age of the child tends to temper *his or her* perceptions of parental symptoms. For example, younger children typically don't have much perspective on relationships and tend to normalize bad parental behavior. As an example, one patient described ongoing parental fights during her elementary school years. "I knew that they were fighting all the time. But that's all I ever knew. They were always fighting. Period. I just assumed that's how parents were. Until they got divorced, when I entered into junior high."

The most obvious victim of the personality disordered parent appears to be the adolescent. Why? Because the adolescent is psychologically mature enough to grasp the basic dysfunctional behavior of the parent, yet feels trapped in a confusing paradox—the parent seems normal but, at the same time, is *not* normal.

Recall that adolescents are attempting to develop into normal healthy adults and are therefore keenly observant of the social rules (even while some may paradoxically rebel against them). The adolescent has accumulated considerable skills of logic during the elementary-school period, and is actively processing and mastering the psychological nuances of social relationships. As a result, the adolescent is particularly challenged by the unexplainable and socially unacceptable behaviors of the personality disordered parent.

Based upon observations in the home, the adolescent may describe his or her parent as phony, insincere, or two-faced. Simultaneously, the adolescent may be fully aware that the parent is well-liked by others, which is seemingly supported by endearing commentaries from colleagues, friends, and clients. "Your father is such a pleasure to work with—we all love his sense of humor!" One patient specifically recalled how frustrated he would become when friends would say, "You're lucky to have such a nice dad!" The patient's father was overly accommodating to visitors yet a virtual nightmare to live with.

The adolescent's confusion is fully understandable. All seems well to the outside world. But when the door to the outside world closes, the destructive parental monster within emerges. So, while the adolescent clearly recognizes the inconsistencies within the parent, he or she can't logically explain the parent's Jekyll-and-Hyde patterns of behavior. The adolescent doesn't know about the phenomenon of personality disorders, which would explain the confusing dichotomy witnessed by the developing adult.

As the adolescent begins to mature and develop a broader and more sophisticated repertoire of social and interpersonal skills, direct conflict is likely to emerge with the personality disordered parent. The adolescent quickly figures out that acceptable social rules do not seem to apply to the parent, or the parent's interaction with them. For example, when confronted by the adolescent, the personality disordered parent is typically impervious to logic. "I am the parent and I can scream, but I will smack you across the mouth if *you* say anything!" "You *will* go to church, but the neighbors will take you. We have other things to do on Sundays." "You better not snoop around my bedroom or office, *ever*! I am the parent! However, I will check your room, cell phone, or e-mail as I see fit." "Don't use drugs! I am an adult so it's okay for me to, but don't *you* use drugs."

Why are the rules of conduct for the young adult versus parent so unbalanced? The answer is fairly simple. The parent has a personality disorder, and all the distortions and deficits that come along with it. These conflicting and turbulent interactions between parent and child may at least partially explain why for some children adolescence is experienced as trying and difficult. It's not necessarily due to their own inherent psychological difficulties (as the cultural stereotype proposes), but rather due to the psychopathology of a personality disordered parent.

When There is More Than One Child

A common observation is that the children of personality disordered parents oftentimes have problematic relationships with each other. For example, the siblings in such families don't seem to develop mutually mature and supportive relationships with each other. Such cases seem a bit perplexing because it seems logical that the offspring of dysfunctional parents might inherently bond together for comfort, commiseration, security, and protection. And, in fact, sometimes they *do* bond together around their shared coping and survival experiences. However, the more frequent pattern seems to be that the siblings are either indifferent or share open conflict with each other. One possible explanation is that dysfunctional parents pit one child against the other. If so, regardless of whether this behavior is intentional, it may account for the ongoing tension among particular siblings.

This pit-one-against-the-other approach to parenting may be fairly obvious. For example, a common example is to compare one sibling to another. "Why can't you be more like your sister, Kellie? Why can't you get good grades like her?"

"Pitting behavior" may also occur implicitly through the development of a "favorite" child. Interestingly, this favored status may be the result of some specific attributes of the child. These attributes are not necessarily positive to anyone other than the personality disordered parent. For example, the favored child may be exceptionally passive (a generally unfavorable characteristic), which enables the pathological parent to establish and maintain control.

It also may be that a specific child is *groomed* to be either the "good child" or the "bad child." The grooming of the "good" child versus the "bad" child is likely to be an outgrowth of the parent's faulty mental processing. Specifically, personality disordered individuals tend to think in extremes (i.e., black and white), much like toddlers. So, outside events and other people are immaturely viewed in absolutes—as either good or bad. With the arrival of children, this identical labeling process kicks in and the personality disordered parent eventually stamps their developing offspring as either good or bad.

How is the assignment of good or bad actually made? The answer probably depends on which particular characteristics and behaviors the personality disordered parent likes/dislikes or approves/disapproves of. Or can take advantage of and *groom*.

For example, a common theme is for the personality disordered parent to gravitate towards the overly compliant child. In this way, the pathological parent can endeavor to get his or her emotional needs addressed by the child—not by a spouse, partner, or peer. Doing so also allows the parent to avoid dealing with other adults, who may expect a healthy give-and-take relationship based upon mutual honesty and vulnerability. Unfortunately, the child is then subsequently cast as confidante and emotional caretaker for the parent (i.e., a "parentalized child"), which usually places the child into a series of ongoing compromises, particularly with the other parent.

Another determinant of whether a particular child is assigned "good" versus "bad" status is the degree to which the child physically resembles a favored or disliked relative. In these cases, the physical similarity facilitates the projection of goodness or badness by the personality disordered parent. The parent may reveal the connection through comments such as, "You're just like your aunt Cecily, and I couldn't stand her!," or "You have so much of your grandfather in you it's almost like he has reincarnated into your body."

It's important to note that the problem with these distinctions among children by a personality disordered parent lies in their extremism. In these families, the good children are perceived as *very* good whereas the bad children are perceived as *very* bad. In the aftermath of incorporating a parental label of either "good" or "bad," individual children may unknowingly accommodate to the parental script. In other words, these children may unconsciously act out the roles assigned to them, so as not to disappoint the projecting parent.

"Something Has Been Taken Away"

As a result of the various psychological deficits encountered in parents with personality disorders, many patients have expressed the existential belief that, "Something has been taken away from me." Upon exploring this concern, many adult children intellectually recognize their parent's psychological dysfunction, but still have difficulty reconciling the situation on an emotional level. They understandably lament the loss of a "good-enough" parent (a parent who is not perfect, but sufficient).

But they also believe that, on some deeper level, *they* have lost a piece of themselves. Most eventually confess that they may never be whole as human beings. They believe that they never had adequate mentors to teach them how to function as adults and how to be complete as individuals. Unfortunately, this belief is genuinely valid. Something *has* been taken away—the right to grow up in a healthy family environment. Fortunately, the right to achieve human hood has *not* been taken away.

While there are many different types and categories of personality pathology, we next consolidate these into two general character styles that probably account for the majority of dysfunctional parenting. These two styles are commonly encountered in clinical practice and consist of (1) the intrusive parenting style and (2) the distant/hostile parenting style. In the next two chapters, these two styles are each outlined in much greater detail.

Chapter 7
The Intrusive Parent

Before discussing the intrusive parent, we must briefly discuss the limitations of breaking people down into "types." There are always downsides or limitations to thinking in terms of *types* of people. One of the most notable is that few people probably ever fit the type completely. In other words, not every descriptor of the type applies to an individual of that type. However, we humans tend to think in terms of types, and doing so allows us to paint a more complete and vivid picture of a particular group. In this chapter, the focus is on describing one of the two types of personality disordered parents that seem to most commonly wreak havoc on their children—the intrusive parent.

Intrusive parents are characterized by their intense emotional and/or physical invasiveness into their children's lives. They engulf their children and persistently overwhelm them on an emotional level as well as on a physical level. To explain and illustrate the dynamics of this personality disordered parenting style, we provide a detailed case example with a subsequent discussion of the representative psychological themes.

This case begins with Ryan, a 22-year-old who had just finished college and was unsure about his career interests. However, his mother Romey was pressuring him to go to law school and become a trial attorney.

A Shattered Childhood

Ryan began treatment by explaining that his mother, Romey, grew up in a small rural town and had known a great deal of hardship during her lifetime. Romey's father was an alcoholic and, although he supported his family through some nonspecific administrative capacity for the town in which they resided, Ryan was under the impression that the locals perceived his grandfather as the proverbial town drunk. On the few occasions that he had had contact with his grandfather, Ryan was never acknowledged by name. Only by "boy." Ryan didn't think that his grandfather actually knew his name.

Romey's mother, Matilda, was a tragic and ephemeral figure. Matilda had contracted a severe case of tuberculosis that was resistant to treatment at the time. Matilda lingered for several years, with her chronic coughing and fatigue, before eventually dying before the eyes of her two young children. Romey was just eight years old at the time of her death. With the death of her mother, Romey was left to be raised by her alcohol-addicted father and her older sister, Hannah, age 10. At this age, abandonment by her mother through death must have been a ghastly loss for Romey—one that likely left a deep emotional dent in her ability to trust and rely on the consistency and availability of others.

Soon after the horrific death of her mother, Romey's father hired a local housekeeper who, from the outset, Romey unequivocally despised. Romey described the housekeeper to Ryan as uneducated, crude, and sexually provocative. Unfortunately, her father's selection of such an individual for employment is probably not that surprising, as individuals with personality disorders oftentimes attract other individuals with dysfunctional personalities.

According to Ryan, soon after the arrival of the housekeeper, the new employee and his grandfather began a torrid sexual affair, which was eventually discovered by the conservative townspeople. Because of the times, the rural setting, and his grandfather's administrative position, there was immense social pressure on the grandfather to wed the housekeeper. Likely due to the fear of losing his subsistent job and meager salary, Ryan's grandfather responded to peer pressure and married the housekeeper, who promptly moved in, bringing along her daughter, Elizabeth.

The new wife unconditionally insisted that Ryan's grandfather eradicate the house of any references to Matilda, including his two young daughters, Romey and Hannah. It's reasonable to assume that Ryan's grandfather had, at least in part, married this woman because he believed that she might raise his daughters. If so, we can imagine that her demands were probably a genuine surprise to him. While Ryan had no explicit information about how this unorthodox request was negotiated, or how Romey and Hannah reacted, we can imagine that they felt angry, displaced, abandoned, and unloved—a second time. In keeping with the wishes of his new wife, the girls' father arranged for them to live with their maternal grandmother, who resided in another state.

Life with Grannie

Several weeks after the marriage of their father, the two girls were unceremoniously shipped to their maternal grandmother. This unexpected and sudden move by the girls resulted in a change of parental figures, schools, friends, and neighborhoods—the loss of all psychosocial stability—shortly following the macabre death of their mother. Like her granddaughters, the maternal grandmother was actively mourning the loss of her daughter, Matilda, as well. According to Ryan's description of this unofficial adoption, the grieving and aging grandmother was fairly displeased about having to take responsibility for her two young grandchildren.

In fairness to Romey's grandmother, she had previously lost a son, and now a daughter, leaving her with only one living child. In the aftermath of these unexpected familial losses, the grandmother appeared to have gradually adapted to life by learning to not attach to others for fear of further loss. Why emotionally invest in other people, such as your granddaughters, and risk yet another unbearable loss? Unfortunately, this approach to loss prevention by the grandmother was not comprehensible to or healthy for Romey and Hannah, who experienced her emotional distance and remoteness as yet another rejection.

The two girls had no choice but to make the best of this difficult transition. They would soon come to understand that the rules in their grandmother's house were going to be far different than those in their father's house.

The girls were now under the supervision of their elderly maternal grandmother, who was a fundamentalist Christian. As such, the grandmother was very strict and conservative in her social, political, and religious beliefs, and absolutely abstained from alcohol. (One wonders how the grandmother felt about her daughter marrying an alcohol addict). Her religious fundamentalism and rigidity were evident in her absolute declarations to the girls that there would be no music or dancing of any kind in the house. In addition, the girls were not allowed to wear make-up at any time. Skirts were to be worn at all times—absolutely no pants— and absolutely below the knee. There were rules upon rules, all apparently geared toward raising good Christian girls, but perhaps not young emotionally needy girls.

Romey and Hannah: Polar Opposites

According to Ryan, the sisters gradually adapted to their new surroundings, but in very different ways, which reflected their uniquely developing personalities. Through the inheritance of temperamental characteristics, their individual experiences in life, and their adaptation to stress, the sisters were developing polar or opposite personality styles. Hannah, as the older sister, surrendered to life in her grandmother's house in a placid and conformist manner. She passively followed the rules and assumed a submissive demeanor. Ryan described her as an adult who lacked energy, ambition, and emotion in her life.

Romey, on the other hand, was like an emotional pit bull—ready to rebel against anyone who attempted to exert control over her. Unlike inert Hannah, Romey was angry, confrontational, and actively on the offense. She was the defiant voice for both sisters, regardless of whether Hannah wanted a spokesperson or not. Romey was aggressive and inflammatory, and her personality structure formed around an oppositional/defiant style of relating to others.

As a young adolescent, Romey acted out her opposition in endless ways. She played music in her room, applied make-up after she got to school, and rolled up her skirts before going to classes. She actively sought out the "tough crowd" at school, and regularly smoked cigarettes with them in a car on the school parking lot. At one point, Romey was confronted by the school principal about her many infractions. He bluntly asked her why she hung out with the wrong crowd, given her superb academic performance? Ryan didn't know how Romey addressed this confrontation with the principal, but she delighted in telling him this story on numerous occasions.

Note that during her early teen years, Romey began to perceive the world as she had experienced her parents—as unavailable, abusive, rejecting, and uncaring. In turn, she seemed to reflect these very feelings outward onto others and reacted by being unavailable, abusive, rejecting, and uncaring to others. She seemed to conclude that if anyone was going to care about her, it would be herself—a belief that was likely the inception of her lifelong self-absorption and narcissism. Even though she appeared superficially intact and was able to maintain a competent façade with regard to her excellent academic performance, Romey's budding personality disorder was resonating with the personalities of her dysfunctional peers.

Dating Days

Ryan indicated that Romey dated quite a bit during her early teen years, even though her grandmother had stipulated that she was far too young to be dating boys. Ryan wasn't sure how Romey managed to evade her grandmother's proscription on dating, but assumed that she frequently lied to the grandmother about her whereabouts and dated under the guise of "going to a friend's house." While we may wonder how Romey was able to execute these forays without getting caught, remember that Romey's grandmother was in mourning and was very self-preoccupied (perhaps depressed?).

Ryan also indicated that the grandmother spent a great deal of time going to local mediums and attending séances in an effort to contact her two dead children. When asked how he knew this, Ryan explained that when he was in grade school and visiting his cousin (Hannah's daughter), the two children discovered in the basement a cardboard box of the deceased grandmother's belongings. (Ryan didn't know the cause of the grandmother's death or how Romey reacted to her passing). The box contained a number of brightly colored turbans. When Ryan's cousin asked Hannah what they were, she replied that they were headdresses worn by the grandmother during séances. (This bit of information suggests that the grandmother was *regularly* participating in séances or perhaps even leading them, given that she had a collection of headwear for such occasions. Note also that there is a potential paradox in the grandmother's behavior: she was a fundamentalist Christian, yet was trying to contact her two dead children through spiritualists.)

So, while the house rules were laid down with absolute fortitude, the house rules were not rigidly enforced, as the grandmother was too emotionally depleted to do so and was oftentimes mentally or physically absent. This discrepancy allowed young Romey to easily undermine the endless rules and to continue in her psychosocial development as an oppositional/defiant personality.

When asked about his mother's dating success, Ryan pointed out that Romey was a very attractive young woman who prided herself in jilting the "nice guys." (This attract/reject pattern is another example of Romey's oppositional/defiant behavior as well as her emotional dishonesty.) Romey seemed to be developing a controlling "I-win-you-lose" quality in her approach to relationships, as if she were re-enacting her own father's unceremonious abandonment of her. She used to regularly brag to Ryan about the fact that she jilted a young man who later owned a Cadillac dealership in her rural hometown. That is, she apparently had jilted the best "catch" in town.

At one point, Romey *intentionally* made two dates for the same night. She kept her date with one of the boys, and while the two sat in a car parked down the street, they heartily laughed as they watched the other date ring the doorbell to Romey's home. The other date was understandably dumbfounded when the befuddled grandmother informed him that Romey wasn't home and wasn't even permitted to date. Romey repeated this contemptible story to Ryan a number of times, particularly when she was intoxicated.

This relished anecdote seems to underscore Romey's early calloused and abusive nature towards others. Was she treating others the way she believed that she was being treated, herself? While it appears on the surface that Romey was confident in maintaining an upper hand over her peers at a fairly early age, in reality, she may have sought out the weak and was terrified by anyone who was psychologically mature (and therefore perceived as a threat to her fragile sense of self).

Married at 16

Consistent with her budding personality disorder, Romey's decision to marry was somewhat precipitous, impulsive, and reactive, and occurred on the heels of her sister's marriage. According to Ryan, Hannah, who was two years older than Romey, met a local bus driver and fell in love. The couple dated for a year and then decided to marry. Hannah's decision to move forward with her life was likely perceived by Romey as yet another abandonment in a long series of abandonments. Romey had first lost her mother to death, then her father to alcoholism and a housekeeper, then her grandmother to grief and apathy, and now Hannah to marriage.

At this point, it is important to note that as a result of their earlier parental losses and subsequent stressful life experiences, Romey and Hannah had cultivated an intense and traumatic bond with each other. This type of enmeshed relationship oftentimes develops between two people within a traumatic context. The bond is based more on shared trauma than similarities and relatedness. Therefore, when Hannah decided to get married, Romey likely experienced this natural development on Hannah's behalf as an intolerable emotional separation or divorce; a divorce from the only human being who had consistently accompanied her on life's treacherous course. Also, by departing through marriage, Hannah left Romey with the grandmother—a situation that Romey was not willing to tolerate.

Shortly after Hannah's marriage, in a fit of opposition and anger, Romey decided that she was going to get married, too, despite being only 16 years old. As one might expect, a teen with these types of loss issues, interpersonal difficulties, and an oppositional/defiant personality isn't likely to make a good marital choice. According to Ryan, she didn't.

Romey met her husband-to-be, Tony, at a local dance. He was 6 years older than her, which should have communicated to Romey that there was a "problem" with him—that he apparently wasn't very successful in dating women in his own age group. Tony danced with Romey, dance after dance, and at the conclusion of the evening, he informed her that she was the girl that he was going to marry. Had Romey been emotionally and psychologically healthy, she might have seen this sort of "fatal attraction" declaration as a red flag. Instead, young Romey went on several more dates with Tony.

Tony was the youngest of eight children in an Italian family, and Ryan suspects that he was essentially forgotten amidst the chaos of so many bodies in a small single household. Tony's mother knew very little English. It was unclear whether this was simply due to a language barrier or an underlying intellectual deficiency (Ryan's grandparents had an arranged marriage and did not know each other before the wedding). Regardless, the eldest sister became the functional mother for this extensive brood. (One can only imagine how ill-equipped and taxed the eldest daughter was with these many children. She was essentially a child mentoring children, which is always an emotionally handicapping situation.)

This dysfunctional household likely contributed to Tony's lack of motivation, particularly in school. He had obtained a high school diploma, but according to Ryan, he had barely gotten through the basic courses and had no plans for further training. After Tony completed high school, he sought employment with few skills and interests, and took a job as a laborer. According to Ryan, Tony was physically unattractive and had very poor social skills.

Ryan explained that his father had always been a loud person. After all, Tony had struggled to have a voice in this frenzied family and, as a result, was very vociferous and argumentative. Ryan believed that this was his father's way of getting attention from his siblings. Ryan went on to describe his father as a "know-it-all," who was prone to rages and needed to be the center of attention. Ryan indicated that his father continually used unsuitable language, frequently with multiple inappropriate words strung together in a single sentence.

To summarize this situation, Romey had apparently discarded all of the acceptable young men in town to hitch up with Tony. Like Romey, he appeared to need a lot of control in his relationships with others, making the Romey/Tony combination a true emotional powder keg. A powder keg that was inherently combustible, according to Ryan. (In looking back at his parents' relationship, Ryan recalled ongoing fights and disagreements between the two of them throughout his childhood and adolescence. Romey and Tony couldn't seem to agree on anything.)

After several dates, Romey and Tony got married. She was 16 and he was 22. They promptly moved away from the small town in which they met. Romey wanted little to do with her grandparents, particularly her grandmother. Like Hannah, she had seized control of her life and had successfully vacated the oppressive atmosphere of her grieving grandmother's house to pursue her own independence and autonomy. What would life hold for her?

Romey and Motherhood

Shortly after marriage, Romey became pregnant with Ryan's older brother, Jason. As Ryan described it, from the time of his departure from the womb, Jason was an unexpected handful. Jason apparently suffered from attention deficit hyperactivity disorder, with an emphasis on hyperactivity. Ryan recalled that Jason was continually "into things." For example, one time Jason painted a neighbor boy's hair with blue wall paint. Another time, he stole a neighbor's "abandoned" dinghy. In keeping with his psychiatric diagnosis, Jason was easily distracted. He might see something happening down the street, run off, and be missing for hours. And then there were innumerable problems at school, including impulsivity, acting out, and poor academic performance.

It is doubtful that Romey was emotionally well-equipped to handle this type of difficult and challenging child. She had spent her life struggling with loss and abandonment, and taking an oppositional stance toward others. She had been forced to take care of her own needs, beginning in childhood, and had never really had the experience of taking care of anyone else's needs. She never babysat a younger sibling or even took care of a pet. Instead, she had become emotionally self-absorbed in an effort to remain protected and safe. However, this wall of protection literally closed her off emotionally from all of those around her, including her children.

Undoubtedly, Jason would have been a handful for any mother, but according to Ryan, Romey simply "threw in the towel" with Jason early on and overly focused her attention on her second son, Ryan, who would seemingly justify her efforts at reproduction. Ryan was born 4 years after Jason and his early memories of childhood were very limited. Ryan recalled a time when Jason was serving him lunch and spit into his milk. He also remembered a Christmas holiday with aunt Hannah's family, when he was probably about 5 years old. He opened up a Christmas gift from Hannah and impulsively stated that it was the wrong toy and not the one that he had requested. Romey responded to this embarrassing public declaration by slapping Ryan squarely across the face, in front of the entire extended family. Ryan recalls that this was a very hard slap—one that left a mark on his face for the better part of an hour. From this embarrassing and painful experience, Ryan learned early on not to challenge Romey, either publicly or privately.

As for Jason, when he entered junior high school, his difficulties continued to mount, from ongoing poor grades to vandalism at school. In response, Romey had to meet with various teachers, go to the principal's office on multiple occasions, and even nullify angry parents who blamed Jason for *their* children's difficulties at school. (We can only wonder how Romey felt about being in the principal's office, again.) As all of this chaos with Jason continued, Ryan was clearly aware that Jason was acting out his role as the "bad son." In contrast, Ryan, who was apparently anxious to avoid any more forceful slaps across the face, took on the role of the "good son."

The Narcotic Years

As Ryan entered the 7th grade, Romey appeared to escalate in her own socially defiant behaviors, but in a rather unexpected way. She began working as a medical assistant in a private physician's office. This position required no particular training other than what was provided by the office nurse. Romey was a quick learner and promptly made a good impression on the physician and staff members (i.e., the façade of competence). She was subsequently given additional responsibilities, which included the ordering of office supplies and medications.

At that time, it was not unusual for physicians' offices to order large stock bottles of common medications, which were dispensed directly to patients rather than using pharmacy prescriptions. As it turned out, ready access to sleeping pills

(Seconal™, a barbiturate) was a temptation that Romey could not resist. Controlled substances. Over the course of time, when Romey ordered a stock bottle of sleeping pills for office use, she simply ordered a second stock bottle for herself—without a prescription.

Romey began recreationally ingesting these powerful drugs on the weekends, remaining in bed and immobilized in a profound drug haze. Romey only left her bed to use the bathroom or fix something for herself to eat. Ryan indicated that she abandoned all housework, the preparation of meals for the family, and even answering the telephone. She was in a virtual drug fog from Friday at 6 pm until Monday morning, when she needed to be ready for work. Ryan vividly recalled the unsettling sight of her torn and disheveled night gown as well as her distinctly odd body odor. (Given her lack of self-care and the fact that she was literally sweating barbiturates, this likely accounted for Romey's unusual body odor.)

As Romey became more tolerant of the drugs, she would attain a state of profound but conscious intoxication and would stagger throughout the house. Romey then developed the intrusive behavior of keeping her family members awake at night with illogical and slurred ranting and ravings. Explicitly, while lying in bed, after the pills took effect, Romey would mumble loudly in an incoherent voice while Tony responded by screaming obscenities at her. During the weekends, this went on for hours throughout the night until Romey exhausted herself and fell into unconsciousness.

While in high school, Ryan recalled that he had an upcoming college placement examination, which was scheduled for a Monday morning. The day before, he pleaded with Romey that he needed to secure a good night's sleep. In response, Romey escalated to new heights that night. She went to the bedroom that Ryan and Jason shared, pounded on the locked door throughout the night (she had previously been intrusive, so the boys locked their door at night), and yelled obscenities at them for hours. Apparently, no one was going to tell Romey what to do or how to behave.

On another occasion, Ryan accompanied Romey to a rheumatology appointment, as she was apparently developing premature arthritis. During this brief visit, the rheumatologist quickly detected Romey's slurred speech and mental incoherence. He cornered Ryan and asked, "What is she *on*?" Ryan was understandably embarrassed. Like a good son, he covered for her with an excuse.

Ryan recalled that he continually worried about Romey overdosing on these drugs and dying. One time, when a friend of Ryan's stopped by the house and rang the front door bell, Romey was collapsed on the floor of the front hallway, only semi-conscious. Ryan quickly rushed her upstairs to avoid discovery, then politely answered the door. As the "good son," Ryan had learned to be compliant and enabling.

Apparently this period of Seconal™ abuse lasted about 10 years, and ended only through the eventual discovery of unaccountable drug orders. The office manager started to notice the invoice sheets, which documented excessive quantities of controlled substances that were not accounted for in the office. An in-office investigation lead back to Romey, who was then promptly fired. Apparently, her employer never pressed legal charges.

With the firing, which was never disclosed to Ryan or Jason at the time (i.e., factual dishonesty), Romey's access to sleeping pills was abruptly halted. Ryan reported that she subsequently went through barbiturate withdrawal, which would be expected. Specifically, he came home from school one day and found Romey lying on her bed, sweating and hallucinating. For hours, she screamed at mirages and cried out to apparitions of deceased family members. The withdrawal process went on for several days, after which Romey proudly affirmed to Ryan, "I got myself off drugs." Apparently, she did.

The Booze Years

Although Ryan indicated that the cessation of barbiturates was a relief for the family, he also reported that the abuse of these drugs was promptly replaced with the abuse of alcohol. (Unfortunately, this replacement or substitution process—i.e., the exchange of one impulsive or addictive behavior for another—is relatively common among individuals with personality disorders.) Ryan candidly admitted that the alcohol abuse, although a problem, was actually a reprieve for the family compared to the sleeping-pill abuse. After excessive drinking, Romey would simply pass out for the night. The entire night. There were no more nightly ranting and ravings on the weekends. There was no more pounding on bedroom doors. Everyone got more sleep.

Around this time, Romey started visiting her ailing alcoholic father. Ryan was required to drive her the seven hours to the grandfather's house, which was located in another state. Of course, the housekeeper-turned-wife had long since divorced Romey's father and he was now dying of complications from alcoholism. At least Ryan assumed that his grandfather was dying of alcoholism. Romey never discussed her father's failing health with Ryan.

During these visits with her father, Romey was the dutiful daughter. She cleaned up the small house he lived in and did the laundry, which was strewn in small piles on the bedroom floor. She then took her father to a local tavern for a drink and helped herself to several as well. Ryan was cast in the role of chauffer. During these visits, the father who had insensitively abandoned his daughters in childhood was addressed by Romey as, "Daddy."

When asked about his relationship with his grandfather during these visits, Ryan indicated that there was *no* relationship. The grandfather was totally self-absorbed. He never even asked Romey about *her* life. The grandfather eventually passed away with little fanfare or acknowledgement. Ryan didn't actually recall any details of his grandfather's death, his mother's reaction to it, or even going to the funeral.

Family Vacations at Aunt Hannah's

Throughout the years, Romey continued to have regular contact with Hannah, despite the two sisters living several states apart. Indeed, the families annually vacationed together. These vacations were uniquely characterized by an escalation in fights between Romey and Tony, just before and during the vacation. It became predictable that Romey would start emotionally igniting Tony the week before a visit with Hannah. By the time the couple arrived at Hannah's house, Romey was supposedly distraught and emotionally shattered from bitter fighting with Tony. Agitated Romey and supportive Hannah would then retreat behind a closed bedroom door and spend hours in isolation. Only as mealtime approached would Romey's tear-soaked body emerge from her burrow with Hannah.

During these visits, Hannah, rather than Ryan, was the receptacle for Romey's many problems, which she tended to externalize and dump onto others. It was Tony's fault. It was Jason's fault. It was her grandmother's fault. It was everybody else's fault. Hannah readily assumed the psychological responsibility of trying to support Romey, perhaps feeling guilty that she had abandoned her younger sister to get married.

Ryan emphasized that this was an invariable vacation pattern that went on for years. Year after year, Romey primed Tony, then the severe fights would break out, and then Romey used Hannah as her emotional reservoir. (We could say that Romey was sadistic in her behavior with Tony and her sons by intentionally and unnecessarily disturbing and disrupting the lives of her family members to remain the center of attention. In addition, she repeatedly engaged Hannah through crisis— behavior that is, again, fairly typical of individuals with personality disorders.)

At this juncture in the story, there is sufficient case material to illustrate several salient features. These features each reflect Romey's personality dysfunction and intrusive parenting style.

Essential Clinical Features

The intrusive parenting style is characterized by the offending parent's continual crossing of emotional and physical boundaries with offspring. As for Romey's relationship with Ryan, she seemed to be emotionally enmeshed with him, beginning in adolescence. He frequently functioned as her confidante (Ryan knew most of her secrets), chauffeur, and drinking escort (Romey had accrued two arrests for driving-while-intoxicated and refused to drive herself to the bars after that). Romey was described by Ryan as very demanding and entitled (i.e., he needed to be continually available to address her needs), yet childlike and dependent (e.g., one time, when Ryan couldn't drive her to the bar because of a previous commitment, Romey didn't talk to him for 2 weeks).

In her relationship with Ryan, Romey repetitively crossed emotional boundaries with her demands and needs around being parented instead of parenting. She wanted to function as the "cared for" in her relationship with her son, not as the "caretaker." This is a common manifestation of boundary violations—parent-child role switching, wherein the child functions as the parent (i.e., the "parentalized child") and the parent functions as the child.

Although not evident in this case, emotional intrusion can also occur when a parent attempts to highjack the child's life experience as his/her own. A number of patients have indicated that, when they were adolescents, their mothers were overly involved with their friends and their social affairs. These mothers seemed to be attempting to reconstruct and repair their own damaged adolescent experiences by reliving them through their children's adolescences.

In addition to the violation of emotional boundaries, parents with intrusive parenting styles oftentimes violate physical boundaries. For example, in Ryan's case, there was evidence of inappropriate physical aggression with Romey's public slap across the face. In addition, there were Romey's repeated attempts of physical invasion of the boys' bedroom when she was intoxicated with barbiturates. As Ryan described it, Romey was physically ever present. She continually commanded attention from others and needed to be the center of everyone's life.

While not present in this case, in some families, physical violation may include ongoing physical abuse and/or sexual abuse. Again, these behaviors within a family are a classic marker for personality dysfunction and are likely to be trans-generational (i.e., exist in generation after generation) in nature.

Other lesser forms of physical violation may include excessive parental expectations around physical development (e.g., early toilet training, expecting children to be overly well-behaved as little ladies and gentlemen) as well as unrealistic demands for physical work to be done by children (e.g., keeping house or doing personal laundry at a young age, building a deck).

Now, let's next examine how Romey displayed the specific characteristics of a personality disordered parent as outlined in the early chapters.

Social Foolers and Outright Liars

On the social surface, in many ways Romey seemed to be just fine. For example, during her high-school days, she achieved excellent grades and exhibited a well-integrated social exterior. Presumably, it was that very competence in academics that led Romey's befuddled principal to confront her about hanging out with "the wrong crowd." As another example of her ability to fool others outside the family, she was able to successfully maintain a position as a medical assistant in a physician's office for many years, while covertly ordering large quantities of controlled substances for personal use. Unfortunately, while she functioned in a responsible position at work, taking care of others and administering treatments, she barely functioned in her own home, where she was frequently oblivious and incoherent in her self-induced stupor. Finally, while her relationship with Ryan was largely self-serving, she appeared to others to be an adequate, if not a good, mother. Romey exemplified the social fooler—seemingly intact on the surface, but highly dysfunctional in the home environment and in close interpersonal relationships.

Dishonesty

Romey was the master of mirage, and mirages require quite a bit of dishonesty to maintain. For example, she had a history of *factual lying* since adolescence. She lied about her whereabouts to her grandmother, dated boys on the sly, and illicitly smoked cigarettes. Later, as an adult, she engaged in a number of addictions, most of which required ongoing lying to conceal their existence or severity. Perhaps the most shocking pattern of lying and deceit was the stealing of controlled substances from her physician-employer's office.

In her interpersonal relationships, Romey was *emotionally* dishonest. She rarely negotiated an emotional need in a sincere and candid fashion, and tended to coerce others into providing what she needed (recall the meltdowns while visiting Hannah?). Her emotional dishonesty was likely a protective mechanism to keep her from getting hurt by others. The cost was a lack of genuine candor in her sticky relationships with others.

Reacting, Not Responding

Another striking clinical feature in Romey's history was her impulsivity as indicated across multiple types of behavior. At various times, she had been addicted to cigarettes, narcotics, and alcohol.

As the years unfolded, Romey began to engage in other types of impulsive behaviors, as well. For example, Ryan described Romey's involvement with "boyfriends" during her marriage to Tony. Ryan actually met one boyfriend—a meeting that was arranged by Romey for reasons Ryan was never able to explain. The boyfriend was, not surprisingly, another alcoholic.

Following a stint of boyfriends, Romey then became addicted to laxatives. Ryan believed that she began experimenting with these products because she had gained a considerable amount of weight with age, despite her longstanding addiction to cigarettes. As a weight-management strategy, she would ingest a large quantity of Ex-Lax™ one hour before eating an excessive amount of food. After the meal, she would immediately retreat to a toilet. When meals were served at Romey's house, this behavior was particularly graphic and upsetting because the bathroom on the main floor of the house was adjacent to the dining room. The laxative abuse went on for years.

It's All About Me, Me, Me

Romey had survived a dreadful childhood in which she had lost her mother to tuberculosis and her father to alcoholism and an affair. She was unexpectedly removed from the family home at an early age and sent to live with a relative stranger, her maternal grandmother. Sadly, her grandmother was immersed in grief, religion, and séances, and not emotionally engaged with either of her two young charges, Romey or Hannah. This series of relational disruptions likely resulted in young Romey coming to the conclusion that, "The only person in this world who is going to take care of me is me." This philosophy formed the foundation for her lifelong self-centeredness and self-absorption. Romey was singularly invested in her own needs and uninterested in the needs of others.

Through a series of disappointing family relationships, Romey was seemingly unable to relate to other human beings in healthy ways for soothing and comfort. Relying on others in this way would have required the development of a genuine relationship, including emotional vulnerability. Instead, she used substances and superficial relationships to meet her needs, neither of which required her to reveal any psychological weakness. Her abuses were private. She managed life on the outside. And, she wasn't reliant on anyone. Ironically, however, Romey *was* reliant on cigarettes, analgesics, alcohol, affairs, and laxatives.

Because of Romey's self-centeredness, even as a child, Ryan had always perceived himself as a burden. Instead of Romey addressing his needs and providing him with a sense of worthiness, she expected Ryan to address *her* needs. According to Ryan, his needs were viewed as unimportant, irrelevant, and unnecessary. He eventually stopped voicing any needs and became, in the aftermath, a very independent individual. Likewise, during sessions, Ryan described his father, Tony, as bored and uninterested in children. Tony never initiated activities with the boys, never chatted with them, or even seemed to like them. Again, they were seemingly viewed as burdens and inconveniences.

Bullies and Victims

We can imagine that Romey would never have agreed that she was a bully. However, recall how in adolescence she laughed at the boy who came to pick her up for a date, while she was sitting in a car with another date? Recall the slap across Ryan's face? Recall the yelling and screaming at her family during periods of intoxication? She consistently manipulated others to meet her own emotional needs, with little in return. If her needs were not promptly addressed, she then threatened to abandon the offenders, particularly Ryan and Tony. This pattern of threatened abandonment is clearly emotional bullying. Overall, she was aggressive and verbally abusive to each and every member of her immediate family. By rarely fulfilling her obligations as a mother and wife, Romey was passive-aggressively telling her family that they were not of importance to her.

"Something Has Been Taken Away"

In what ways might Ryan have been affected by growing up with a personality disordered parent of the intrusive type? During sessions, Ryan always described feeling "empty." He believed that his role in relationships was to fully accommodate a partner and to have no personal needs, himself—a very unfulfilling way to experience relationships. Therefore, relationships turned out to be quite a lot of work for him. He was fearful that he would never be able to execute the relationship process correctly, based on his dysfunctional experiences with Romey and Tony. This theme is a repeated concern among patients with caretakers who have personality disorders.

Chapter 8
The Distant-Hostile Parent

In the previous chapter, we discussed the first of the two distinct parenting styles related to personality pathology, the intrusive parent. Recall that the intrusive parenting style is characterized by emotional, and even physical, invasiveness of the child. In this chapter, we introduce a second general parenting style—the distant-hostile parent. In this style of parenting, the personality disordered parent is predominantly aloof, emotionally disengaged, and under-involved. Such parents may be angry, antagonistic, and intimidating as well, but they lack the emotional stickiness seen with the intrusive parenting style.

To explain and illustrate the dynamics of this personality disordered parenting style, we provide a detailed case example with a subsequent discussion of the representative psychological themes. This case begins with Katherine, who began psychotherapy when she was about 28 years old but continued treatment intermittently for years. At the time of the initial consultation, she was nearing the completion of a residency in internal medicine and was struggling in her relationships with males. This concern provided a clinical doorway to Katherine's relationship with her father, Richard, a personality disordered parent of the distant-hostile type.

Humble Beginnings

Katherine's father, Richard, grew up in a small, Midwest, rural farming community. Richard's father supported the family through farming a few acres of land and a full-time position with an oil company. While not poor, the family had to be extremely mindful of spending in order to maintain their upper position in the lower class. Still, in this rural Wisconsin community, few had a better standard of living.

Richard had a younger brother, Gene, and although Katherine was uncertain about their specific age difference, Gene seemed to have been a few years younger than Richard. Gene unexpectedly died around age 2 or 3 years, supposedly by accidental drowning. However, the family whisperings around the specific circumstances of

Gene's death were ominously inconsistent; the storyline shifted, depending upon who was sharing the account. According to some family members, the drowning occurred in a lake. Others were convinced that the fateful incident occurred in a water well. Some family members implied that Richard might have pushed Gene into the lake or water well. Other family accounts indicated that Richard was not at fault, but perhaps remiss in not adequately watching over or rescuing Gene. Whatever the version, the issue of accountability for Gene's death was squarely placed upon Richard, who would have been no more than 5 or 6 years of age at the time.

Katherine never felt comfortable directly exploring the circumstances of this tragic incident with her family, especially with Richard or her paternal grandmother. Understandably, the family never openly discussed Gene's death. However, as far back as Katherine could remember, Richard assumed the guilt for the death of his younger brother. Katherine's mother, Phyllis, privately affirmed that Richard did indeed feel responsible for Gene's death.

Regardless of the specifics of the accident, it sounded as though one fact was clear: two young children were playing near a lake or a water well without adult supervision. When explicitly asked why the two boys were not being monitored by an adult, Katherine was somewhat startled by the query, indicating that she had never considered this aspect of the incident. She, of course, didn't know the answer. However, the question led Katherine to a discussion about Richard's mother, Vera.

Katherine's initial description of Vera focused on her physical appearance. Apparently, Vera was extremely obese. Katherine explicitly recalled the rolls of fabric that covered her grandmother's body. While not uncommon today, in those times, obesity was extremely unusual—i.e., a peculiar and outlying medical malady, particularly in a hardworking farming community.

Katherine then focused on her grandmother's teeth, which she described as crooked, erratic, and asymmetrical. Vera's haphazard teeth, coupled with her long narrow nose, gave her a somewhat wicked appearance. However, according to Katherine, she was not at all malicious or unkind, but rather aloof and emotionally disengaged (which may explain why the boys were left unattended that fateful day).

Katherine also emphasized that her grandmother had few interests and lacked any zest in life. Perhaps this was due to her morbid obesity. If so, she may have been under-involved with her children because she couldn't *physically* meet the challenges. Indeed, as a small child, Katherine recalled taking trips with her grandmother to the local zoo. Upon their arrival, Vera promptly took a seat on the closest bench and encouraged Katherine to wander around the zoo and see the animals—without her.

When asked about the relationship between Vera and Richard, Katherine described it as very superficial and distant, even disconnected. Apparently, this was not an unusual stance for Vera, who Katherine described as fairly superficial, shallow, unsophisticated, and unimaginative. It was as if Vera went through the motions of life, but did not emotionally participate in her daily experiences. Accordingly, Katherine had a very difficult time socially engaging with her grandmother, who frequently used guilt to coerce her busy granddaughter into visiting. Such visits were uncomfortable for Katherine, and apparently never long enough for her grandmother. Each visit would predictably end with, "Can't you stay longer?," despite an hour or two of literally vacant conversation.

Given Vera's penchant for using guilt on others, a new interpretation of Gene's tragic death emerged. Did Vera project her own guilt about Gene's death onto Richard, unfairly blaming him for *her* irresponsibility. Realistically, she was responsible for the boys and their care that fateful day, not Richard, who was barely of school age. At the time of this tragic incident, did she respond to it by influencing the subsequent interpretation of the circumstances, so that she was absolved of any accountability? It wasn't her fault, the adult. It was Richard's fault. It was the child's fault. If this premise is true, then Vera intentionally saddled young Richard with an onerous and dreadful burden, so that she could absolve herself of any culpability.

Whatever the circumstances, Richard completely absorbed the responsibility for his younger brother's death and lived with that guilt throughout his lifetime. As a result, this incident likely had a long-lasting and devastating impact on his self-esteem and self-concept.

The next major event in Richard's life was his sexual molestation by a male farm hand during early adolescence. While Katherine was not privy to the explicit details of this experience, the molestation apparently was not a single incident. Richard never discussed this experience with Katherine, except on one occasion during an argument. It was only in the heat of the moment that this bit of information was unintentionally disclosed. Richard angrily commented that, "My father would have killed him (the farm hand) if he knew about this!"

The final major event in Richard's young life was the family's decision to sell the farm and relocate to a nearby city. This decision was precipitated by his father's job transfer with the oil company. While a relocation of this type might spell opportunity for a child from an impoverished rural community, Richard was highly reluctant to move with his family. After some discussion with his parents, it was decided that Richard would remain in this rustic community and finish high school. He would stay with friends while his family relocated to a city approximately 100 miles away.

You're in the Army Now

Following graduation from high school, Richard enlisted in the army. The context of this decision has been lost in time. Perhaps it was an opportunity to fully emancipate from his family-of-origin. Perhaps it was a vehicle to see the world. Perhaps it was viewed by Richard as an opportunity to gain more life experience. Whatever the reason, it naturally resulted in less contact with Vera, which may have been a primary motivation. After all, according to Katherine, Richard always intensely disliked his mother's appearance. She was a total embarrassment to him. (As Vera was obese during a time when there were few obese people, she must have been fairly conspicuous at social gatherings, which genuinely and understandably humiliated young Richard.)

Apparently, Vera's weight wasn't the only personal characteristic that mortified Richard. He was also ashamed of her poor language skills and grammar, which were the legacy of an impoverished childhood. While Richard was in the army, he sent Vera a book on the proper execution of the English language. Apparently, he was hoping that she would take an interest in self-improvement. When he returned home on leave, he asked her if she had read the book. Based on what we know about Vera's low energy and lack of involvement in life, it's no surprise that she didn't touch the book. Richard was infuriated. In the aftermath of this incident, Vera's poor speech remained an unspoken bone of contention in their relationship.

Richard's stint in the army was characterized by two additional details that reflect his underlying personality structure. First, Richard periodically wrote his parents letters containing explicit instructions for very specific supplies. For example, on several occasions, he indicated that he needed a special type of writing paper, and would carefully clarify the dimensions and texture of the paper he wanted. He also specified what type of writing paper he *didn't* want. He was very particular, fussy, and finicky. Indeed, most of the content of his letters were in this vein—clarifying what he needed to have sent to him. How did Katherine know about her father's writing demands? Apparently, following the death of her paternal grandmother, Katherine discovered some letters that were written by Richard to Vera during his army days. The content was unemotional, non-relational, and non-intimate. There wasn't even any discussion of his experiences in the army. Richard focused primarily on what he needed from Vera—in concrete detail.

In addition to his fussiness about personal needs, a second indication of Richard's underlying personality dysfunction was his unusual nickname in the army: "Snake" (as in "snake in the grass"). Katherine had no idea why he was nicknamed Snake. Was this nickname because Richard could craftily maneuver situations and procure illegitimate items that others couldn't? Whatever the reason, it is doubtful that Snake was a nickname of endearment or genuine respect.

By the completion of his two-year stint in the army, it sounded as though Richard was clearly developing into a narcissistic individual. Typically, narcissism develops out of parental under-involvement and detachment. Although many details are missing about Richard's developmental history, Vera's emotional under-involvement is one factor that painfully stands out. So, at an early age, it's likely that Richard recognized that the only person who was going to meet Richard's emotional needs was Richard. No one else was going to, and certainly not Vera. The evolution of this type of attitude tends to result in the development of a self-serving and interpersonally manipulative individual. From another perspective, the evolution of this type of personality structure might be seen as an *adaptation* to parental under-involvement and emotional neglect.

College, Marriage, and Children

Following his stint in the army, Richard took full advantage of the GI bill, which essentially provided a free college education to ex-military personnel. Richard went to a local college, performed unexpectedly well, and decided to go to medical school. While Katherine had no idea how well Richard academically performed in medical school, he must have been innately intelligent to have successfully met the educational demands of such training. Richard successfully graduated, completed a one-year internship, and then began his medical practice.

During medical school, Richard met Katherine's mother, Phyllis, at a dance. Phyllis was a dark-haired, blue-eyed, elongated beauty, who came from a nearby rural town. She was studying to be a nurse. Oddly, after only three dates, Richard and Phyllis made the *intellectual* decision to get married. Katherine indicated that Richard oftentimes referred to their brief courtship and decision to get married as if it were a business negotiation, relatively devoid of any emotion. Again, given Richard's narcissistic personality, it probably *was*, to some degree, a business negotiation. Richard wanted to be married and Phyllis wanted to have children. And, they shared a number of things in common. They both came from rural towns in the same state. They both were in the medical field. They both were practical, no-nonsense people. Apparently it was time to get married, so they did.

At the onset of Richard's medical career, the young couple decided that it was time to begin a family. Unexpectedly, Phyllis had extreme difficulty getting pregnant and suffered repeated miscarriages. At the time, there weren't the advanced fertility treatments that are available today. So, the couple struggled on, year after year, and hoped for a successful pregnancy. When Phyllis finally managed a viable pregnancy, she was thrilled. Richard seemed pleased but was busy cultivating a successful medical practice. After a full nine-month gestation, without any medical complications, Phyllis gave birth to a healthy son. Although the boy had a formal name, the couple promptly nicknamed him, "Butchie."

From the outset, Butchie was a bit of a management problem. He seemed to have inherited a high degree of innate impulsivity and continually struggled with controlling his own behavior.

Whether this was fully the case, or whether his exceptionally bright parents expected too much out of their first child, is unknown. Still, according to Katherine, Phyllis was continually frustrated with Butchie's inability to follow rules and directions, and frequently called him, "Stupid." (Indeed, "Stupid" was used so frequently by Phyllis that it seemed to be Butchie's second nickname.)

Phyllis was a no-nonsense kind of mother. She was comfortable with structure and readily laid down the rules. But, apparently, even *she* had difficulty shaping young Butchie into a well-regulated adult. So, a family pattern developed in which Phyllis initially disciplined Butchie for his infractions, then Richard would return home from work and provide the finishing lesson with a belt. Katherine recalled hearing the beatings of her older brother and his screaming, but she could not explicitly recall what he had done to deserve this degree of punishment.

Katherine came along nine years after Butchie. Phyllis was thrilled to have a second child, even though Butchie had thoroughly exhausted her. Unlike Butchie, Katherine was contemplative, bright, self-sufficient, and low-maintenance—the type of child that Phyllis would naturally attach to.

Katherine rigidly followed the rules, didn't have to be told multiple times to do chores, and entertained herself by making mud pies in the backyard. As a result, Katherine was the proverbial "good child" whereas Butchie was designated as the "bad child."

Katherine's early history contained one additional dynamic. When Katherine was about 6 years old, an older male relative began to sexually molest her on a regular basis. With this development, Katherine became very socially withdrawn. She would oftentimes sleep in a chair, downstairs, to avoid this relative, who would stay during his visits in a bedroom that was upstairs and across the hall from hers. Phyllis and Richard never asked Katherine why she retreated to the downstairs at night, where their bedroom was located. The sexual abuse continued until this relative relocated out-of-state, when Katherine was about 9 years old. For Katherine, his departure was a reprieve.

Poor Me, Poor Me, Pour Me a Drink

During her high-school years, Katherine recalled that her father was a daily heavy drinker. He would routinely have a martini or two before dinner, and then several beers after dinner. Every evening without fail. To win favor with her aloof and emotionally disengaged father, Katherine would oftentimes mix his martinis, gently shaken with a hint of vermouth. It was a way for her to share some type of social experience with her father. As his addiction to alcohol progressed, Katherine noticed that her father ended most evenings by "sleeping" in his favorite chair in the living room. Reflecting back, with more life experience, she realized that he simply passed out most nights.

In addition to these martini rituals, father and daughter routinely shared a sterile bedtime ritual. Before heading off to bed, Katherine went to Richard. Not for a good-night kiss, but to shake his hand, which Richard insisted upon. It was a good-night hand shake. Richard was very specific that Katherine *not* squeeze his hand. He repeatedly informed her that he might have to do minor surgery the next day. "I'm a doctor!," he would exclaim.

By the completion of high school, Katherine and Richard shared little beyond nightly handshakes. In fact, he had had little to do with her during her entire lifetime. Katherine always rationalized that his lack of emotional availability and time with her was due to his extensive workload. After all, he was a very busy and well respected physician. His patients seemed to adore him, and his colleagues seemed to highly respect him. Richard understandably worked long hours, underwent the rigors of being on call, and delivered babies at all hours of the night. So, Katherine naturally assumed that Richard was emotionally absent because of his demanding career.

To further complicate their father-daughter relationship, Katherine was keenly fearful of men. Because the older male relative had sexually molested her for 3 years during her childhood, she now envisioned men as predatory. They were to be feared. Given Richard's remote and antagonistic personality, it's no wonder that Katherine was hesitant to approach him.

Richard's Hot Buttons

During therapy sessions, Katherine underscored that her father was always very negative and antagonistic. His antagonism towards others manifested in a number of curious ways, some dating back to adolescence. For example, one hot button with Richard was "fat people." Richard could not stand obese individuals, and within the confines of the family home, he regularly proclaimed his disgust of them.

Another hot button for Richard was the proper execution of the English language. He meticulously pointed out grammatical errors in the local newspaper as well as the speech errors of those around him. He would become completely obsessed with one particular infraction for weeks at a time, ruminating about the insult to his ears. In addition, Richard would become obsessed with the novel pronunciation of a word. For example, he ruminated for weeks on the "correct" pronunciation of the word "scone" (phonetically pronounced "skone") as "skane."

Yet, another hot button for Richard was the local construction of a new hospital, which was approximately two miles from the family home. Richard eventually joined the staff of the new hospital, which resulted in a very convenient drive to work for him, yet he initially and adamantly opposed the construction of the hospital. Katherine did not recall exactly why he was opposed to the new construction, but she did recall intoxicated rants, during which Richard referred to the hospital founders as "liars and cheats." "They're all liars and cheats. Liars and cheats. All of 'em." Apparently, this private assault on the hospital administration was a repetitive theme for Richard and it went on for years.

As another example, at his favorite hospital, which was located in an urban area, Richard was known as a maverick and a rebel. He would promptly latch onto any political issue like an angry bull terrier, sinking his teeth into any controversy that had meaty substance. For example, he was adamantly opposed to the doctors eating in the public cafeteria at the hospital. They were physicians, and physicians needed a private dining room. With all of his political prestige and emotional fortitude, Richard led the physician troops to victory by pressuring the hospital into constructing a private dining room for "doctors only." What struck Katherine was Richard's unbridled anger and vigorous entitlement. Her father's vehemence towards the hospital during these negotiations was frightening.

As a final example of hot button issues, the city was contemplating the construction of a new stretch of freeway. The new expressway would facilitate the flow of traffic from the congested southern suburbs to the northern areas of the city, where there was a large university as well as access to an interstate freeway. Most of the locals were highly in favor of the new road segment, because it would morph a convoluted drive on the backstreets into a fast-paced highway route. Richard was absolutely infuriated with the proposed highway, which he considered totally unnecessary. He believed that the sole purpose of the new freeway segment was to facilitate the shopping trips of the local wealthy women to a larger adjacent city. He hatefully referred to the freeway as "Rich Bitch Avenue."

Holding Court

Richard had always had an innate fondness for England. He liked British architecture, the precision of the King's language, and the cozy pubs. Perhaps his passion for the United Kingdom was also stimulated by their well-established monarchy. Whatever the reason, Katherine clearly indicated that her father loved to emulate these monarchs and "hold court." When asked what she meant by this term, Katherine indicated that her father relished being the center of attention (literally, in the center) and dominating social situations, particularly when intoxicated.

111

As an example, throughout his marriage, Richard had the arrogant presumption to dominate entire family meals with sophisticated medical talk. Even as small children, the entire discussion around the family dinner table focused on Richard and his patients. Katherine indicated that these were not casual discussions of unusual or interesting medical events, or entertaining characters in his practice. These presentations were more like stately grand lectures, with discussions of detailed medical evaluations, consideration of various complex diagnoses, and reviews of complicated interventions and treatments. She never understood what he was talking about. Of course, Katherine and Butchie said little-to-nothing during these family meals, whereas Phyllis offered some occasional commentary from a nursing perspective.

Then there were the surgeries. Because of the intense social attention, Richard genuinely enjoyed the occasional elective surgery he underwent as a patient. He always took residence in his favorite hospital, always received a private VIP room, and always basked in the attention of his various visitors, including fellow physicians who stopped by to see how he was doing. Like the family dinners at home, Richard dominated these conversations with visitors, expounding on his laboratory reports, obtuse surgical findings, and amounts and types of administered intravenous fluids.

Holidays were another pivotal time for royal Richard. During the holidays, Phyllis would dutifully retrieve Richard's parents by driving the 100-mile one-way distance to pick them up. Katherine indicated that her grandparents were not very verbally interactive with Richard and Phyllis during these holiday visits, but rather assumed their seats in the formal living room and looked like emotionally vacant wax figures. In contrast, even though he disliked his parents, Richard "entertained" his family during these sittings with more intellectualizations around his medical practice. Richard was in control, Richard would set the pace for the evening, and Richard would be the center—whether or not anyone could appreciate his at-home medical lessons. After sharing the holiday meal, Richard would retreat to his high-backed formal chair in the living room (his throne?), spending the rest of the evening suckling Scotch and reading the local newspaper, which served as a convenient barrier to further interaction with others.

Katherine recalled a particular incident that occurred at her wedding. Prior to the wedding,

Richard fervently groused about the cost. He *never* expressed any satisfaction that his daughter had found a life partner and was happy. He focused only on the money involved. It was the cost of the wedding dress. It was the cost of the open bar. It was the cost of the reception. Katherine recalled feeling guilty that her physician father was so stressed about her wedding, even though he regularly had lobster flown in from New England for his own dinners.

Following the reception, both sides of the couple's family retreated to the same local hotel. Katherine took her new husband to the suite that was rented by her father for an after-reception gathering. When they entered the suite, they saw some 20 relatives lined up, and sitting silent and somber, with their backs against the walls. Meanwhile, Richard danced in the middle of the room with a lampshade on his head and a drink in his hand. Katherine was shocked and embarrassed. In contrast, Richard seemed delighted to be the center of the festivities.

Katherine's Medical School and Residency Years

Perhaps to win her father's attention and/or to bolster her own faltering sense of self-confidence, Katherine decided to go to medical school. She had achieved excellent grades in college, yet the competition for entry into medical school was particularly fierce the year that Katherine applied. When she was accepted to a prominent medical school, the one that her father had been trained at, Richard was completely unresponsive. He offered not one word of congratulations nor any acknowledgement of her achievement. Katherine was genuinely surprised by his lack of response. She had hoped that he would be pleased. After all, those medical discussions around the dining room table had successfully culminated in her own entry into medical school. Rather than being pleased and proud, Richard seemed aloof and threatened. From a narcissistic perspective, he now had to share center stage with his daughter, and that was *not* going to be acceptable.

During medical school, Katherine developed a relatively minor difficulty with her knee. The proper treatment would have been to use a knee brace during periods of vigorous activity in conjunction with strengthening exercises. When Katherine disclosed the results of her consultation with an orthopedic specialist at her medical school, Richard promptly scoffed at and dismissed the specialist. He arranged for Katherine to have a consultation with a second orthopedics specialist, an old crony of his, in their much smaller hometown. To Katherine's surprise, this specialist recommended extensive knee surgery, including the removal of her knee cap. This extensive surgery would entail a full leg cast for 6 weeks. Katherine was understandably surprised by this dramatic recommendation, which starkly contrasted with the opinion of the specialist at her own university. However, Richard was adamant about the surgery. His colleague was the "best in the field" and she needed to have the surgery. Katherine reluctantly agreed to undergo the surgery, which in the aftermath entailed dragging a heavy cast around for several weeks and then undergoing physical therapy for three months—all during the rigors of medical training. It was grueling for her.

Several weeks after presenting this vignette in therapy, Katherine expressed her anger towards her father for pushing her to have the knee surgery during medical school. It had been a true hardship for her during the demands of training. Then Katherine made a shocking statement. She stated, without any prompting, that Richard may have pushed this unnecessary and debilitating surgery upon her to sabotage her success at medical school. As shocking as this accusation was, it raised legitimate questions. Why were the two orthopedists' opinions so divergent? Why did her father elect a consultation with an old crony when there were younger and more competent surgeons in town? Why did the surgery, which was elective in nature, have to be done while Katherine was in medical school? Was this simply poor judgment on Richard's part, or was this a selfish means of eliminating the competition? Could there only be *one* doctor in the household?

At the time that Katherine disclosed her thoughts about the possibility of an unnecessary surgery and Richard's possible intent of eliminating the competition, the infamous childhood incident entailing the drowning of Gene re-surfaced. Was it at all possible that Richard had actually eliminated the competition, far earlier, and that Gene's drowning was truly no accident? We will never know.

In the middle of processing the knee-surgery incident, Katherine brought up in session a complicated medical case of hers, in which the patient had unexpectedly died. Katherine was unprepared for the patient's death and blamed herself, rather than the unexpected change in the course of the patient's illness. She commented that, after the incident, she had called her father for support. (It was somewhat surprising that she did this, as she rarely initiated contact with him.) She presented the case to him, detail by detail, and when she was finished, there was a long pause. Then Richard glibly responded, "Well, you killed him." It was a shocking comment. Through a review of the case by supervisors and peers, it was patently clear that she had not killed the patient (she was the resident—one of the lower-level professionals on a large treatment team), nor had anyone else on the treatment team. However, Richard quickly blamed Katherine for the patient's death, as if to punish her for being a caring and compassionate physician.

As for a final incident during residency, Katherine found herself in need of a car for transportation to work. While she was paid a modest salary, she hardly had the funds to purchase a car. She discussed the situation with her father. He advised her to take out a loan and buy a good used car. She located a reliable used car and agreed to apply for a loan from the local bank. However, on the day of the bank negotiation, Richard ambushed her with the idea that *he* take out the loan. Katherine could then pay him back through monthly payments with interest and he would have a tax write-off. Katherine felt that she had no choice but to agree. In the aftermath, however, she concluded that she couldn't afford the higher monthly payments to her well-heeled physician father. So, Katherine had to take out a personal loan at a much higher interest rate in order to pay him back. Richard's self-serving behavior was becoming more evident to Katherine.

The Grand Medical School Reunion

Going to medical school is certainly an honor and a privilege. In an uncanny fashion, Katherine and her father had shared that same unique experience by attending and graduating from the identical medical school exactly 30 years apart. This meant that they were destined to share but one medical school reunion together before Richard retired. At the time of this exceptional reunion,

Katherine was living out-of-state with her husband. She looked forward to the medical school reunion and proudly commented about the family legacy to her local friends—two doctors, the same medical school, exactly 30 years apart. Katherine had arranged with her mother for everyone in the family to meet during the reunion.

When Katherine and her husband arrived in town for the reunion, they went directly to her parents' motel room. With coat in hand, Phyllis greeted them outside of the motel room and suggested that they immediately go to lunch. Phyllis never invited the couple into the hotel room. Katherine asked where her father was, and Phyllis tersely responded that he was tied up with the big football game, which coincided with the medical school reunion. Katherine assumed that there would be time, later, to see her father, take photographs in front of the school, and commiserate about their medical school days. Katherine especially wanted a photograph of the two of them, father and daughter, in front of the medical school's famous courtyard statue.

After lunch, which was quite pleasant, the couple dropped Phyllis off at the motel. That was the last that Katherine saw of either of her parents during the medical school reunion weekend. Following the event, Katherine telephoned her mother. During their conversation, Phyllis unintentionally revealed that Richard had not actually *attended* the game. He had been in the motel room *watching* the game. He couldn't walk to the door of the motel room to greet his daughter, who had just arrived from another state—nor make any plans to see her during the visit.

The Abuse Disclosure

After Katherine got married (shortly after residency), she decided to disclose to her father that an older male relative had molested her. This decision came about because Katherine found herself increasingly uncomfortable at large family functions when this relative was in attendance. He was many years older than Katherine, and now divorced from a woman who was 15 years younger than him. Oddly, despite both being adults, the male relative continued to treat Katherine like a child. He even called her by the childhood nickname that he had used when he was molesting her. It was far too uncomfortable for Katherine to be around him, so she reflexively avoided family functions to minimize her contact with him. She wanted to share this dilemma with her father, and thereby explain her absences at family gatherings.

Katherine elected to save this delicate discussion with her father for a time when they would not be interrupted. She knew that Phyllis always went to her hairstylist on Thursdays. So, Katherine scheduled a visit with her father on a Thursday, but did not reveal its purpose. Shortly after her arrival to the house, Katherine began her painful disclosure. She revealed that this man had molested her for 3 years. She explained that having contact with him now stimulated horrible memories for her. She hoped that her father would understand why she was avoiding contact with the family—that she was really avoiding contact with this particular relative, not Richard or Phyllis.

As Katherine disclosed this intimate history to Richard, he became angrier and angrier. At first, she thought that he was appropriately angry with the male relative. But he wasn't angry at the relative – he was angry at Katherine! He promptly screamed at her to "sit," like one commands a dog. Richard then yelled, "He didn't penetrate you did he?," as if to excuse the three years of sexual and emotional trauma that Katherine had endured. It was at this point that Richard angrily revealed his own history of sexual abuse by the farm hand, and screamed, "Sexual abuse happens in all families!" His message was clear: "Get over it and don't bother me with it."

Katherine was understandably shocked by her father's response. She was hurt, humiliated, and re-traumatized. This disastrous encounter was the beginning of the end of her relationship with her father. Richard had, yet again, marginalized her. He had, again, invalidated her. However, Katherine was now an adult. She was no longer a passive little girl naively seeking approval from her father. She was a competent adult woman, on an equal professional par with her father, yet she was being treated like an inconvenient and burdensome child.

The Big Downsize

Shortly after an intense and ravaging illness, Phyllis unexpectedly passed away. Richard promptly decided to downsize his living circumstances. Katherine and Butchie were never actually notified of his plan to downsize. They still had belongings in the family home. However, one day, Leslie, Butchie's daughter from his former marriage to an alcoholic, contacted Katherine and indicated that Richard had moved. In the process, Richard had thrown out all of Katherine's remaining personal belongings, dropped off excess furniture to the local Goodwill, and moved the remainder of his belongings into a small house. Katherine explicitly asked Leslie about her scrapbooks and personal items—things that were left in the attic. Leslie responded that *everything* had been thrown away.

Again Katherine was emotionally stunned by her father's lack of empathy or caring. It was about this time that Katherine and her husband moved to yet another state to advance their careers. Her relationship with her father was virtually nonexistent by that point.

Richard passed away about five years after Phyllis. Although he had always professed it vitally important that he leave some inheritance to his children, he didn't leave a dime to either Butchie or Katherine. Instead, he donated the money to two charities that he had little association to—perhaps as a final arrogant slap in the face to the children who had disappointed him.

The Distant-Hostile Parenting Style

As described at the beginning of this chapter, the distant-hostile parenting style is characterized by parental aloofness, emotional disengagement, antagonism, intimidation, and a lack of empathy. Note that Richard was rarely directly intrusive. While there were infrequent occasions when he violated boundaries (e.g., Katherine's knee surgery), he generally maintained an aloof, uninvolved, and angry emotional position with her. In his relationships with others, he consistently remained focused on *his* needs, which were always seen by him as preeminent. He was easily threatened by others (e.g., Katherine and her achievement of being a physician) and was consistently disinterested in the needs and feelings of others. The major themes in Richard's psychological life were extreme self-centeredness coupled with pervasive hostility.

Social Foolers and Outright Liars

Richard was clearly an adept chameleon and easily able to fool others. On a surface level, he apparently portrayed himself to his patients, medical colleagues, and office staff as a caring, compassionate, and concerned physician. However, in the home environment, Richard was just the opposite. He was self-centered, insensitive, controlling, and detached. Through his every action and statement, he was pervasively angry and petulant. He seemed to intensely dislike people, particularly his own family members. Particularly his own mother, Vera. To the outside world, Richard appeared to be successful, talented, and a valuable member of the community. On a personal level, he was angry and immature, doggedly pursuing his own needs to the exclusion of the needs of others. So, there is clear evidence of a social paradox.

Like most children of a personality disordered parent, Katherine was confused by her father's pathology. He was bright and successful. He seemed to be highly respected by his colleagues and patients. Yet, her relationship with him was troubled, disconnected, and distressing. So, at the outset, she assumed that *she* must be "the problem." As a child, how could she have been expected to recognize her father's pathology?

We might also say that Richard was a master of emotional dishonesty. The only emotions that he regularly expressed to his intimates were anger, jealousy, and threat. Katherine could not recall a single tender moment between the two of them, a single positive feeling expressed towards her, or an affirmation of praise to anyone in the family. Like the hospital officials and the city planners who riled Richard's anger, his family members were likely all evil-doers who constantly opposed his will, as well. From a clinical perspective, Richard displayed a characteristically singular range of negative emotions so commonly encountered among those with particular personality disorders.

Reacting, Not Responding

Richard clearly was a reactive individual. He reacted, rather than responded, to Butchie's behavior (the beatings with a belt), the hospital's hesitancy to build a private dining room for the physicians, the construction of a local hospital, and Katherine's disclosure of sexual abuse. Indeed, Katherine did not present any recollections that reflected genuine responding. Unfortunately for his family, Richard's prominent reactive emotion was clearly anger.

It's All About Me, Me, Me

Perhaps the most prominent personality disorder feature that Richard displayed was his intense self-absorption. Richard only seemed to be able to process experiences from a self-perspective—how things affected him, what they meant to him, and what the outcome would be for him. He didn't seem genuinely capable of processing experiences from the perspective of another individual. This is what is termed in the mental health field as an "empathic failure with others."

This inability to empathize or emotionally connect with others likely relates to his early upbringing. Recall that Vera was very self-absorbed and emotionally remote. Vera was physically present, but in Richard's eyes, she was not a competent mentor. She was obese. She was slovenly. She couldn't speak the King's English correctly. She didn't protect Gene and Richard at the lake/water well. Then there was Richard's father, who was virtually non-existent, perhaps due to working two jobs—the farm and the oil company. In addition, Richard had no living siblings. These bits of information suggest that Richard grew up in a very emotionally sterile environment. As a result, he had no emotional mentoring from experienced and mature adults. He was literally not taught compassion or how to emotionally experience others. It was all about Richard. It had to be for him to survive.

Because of his intense self-centeredness, both Butchie and Katherine were perceived by Richard as burdens. Butchie was hardly the son that a narcissistic high-achiever would desire. Butchie was impulsive and impetuous. Butchie wasn't as bright as Richard. Butchie required ongoing discipline. Butchie was embarrassing to Richard. First, Richard had to contend with an obese mother with poor language skills. And now Butchie.

Katherine was a different story. She had her mother's beauty—long, dark, thick hair; piercing blue eyes; and a regal elongated figure. In addition, she had an amazing intellect, even as a child. She would certainly be the child that someone like Richard would be proud of. Instead, Richard was deeply threatened by her. She, too, was a burden, but in a completely different way than Butchie. Katherine was capable of great things, which threatened Richard's role as the head monarch in the family home.

Bullies and Victims

Richard was, without a doubt, a bully. He bullied his mother about her grammar. He bullied Butchie with multiple beatings, rather than getting him to a therapist. He bullied his family with his medical discourses at the dinner table. He bullied Katherine into having a debilitating knee surgery while in medical school. He bullied the hospital administration so that he could sit with his equals in a splendorous hospital-sponsored dining club. He bullied the community with his opinions about "Rich Bitch Avenue." Overall, Richard was an unrelenting bully who delighted in being superior to others.

"Something Has Been Taken Away"

Not surprisingly, Katherine always felt unwanted by her father. She also always felt somehow responsible for the dysfunction in their relationship. To compound matters, she had been sexually abused by a male relative, which further compromised her ability to trust males. In therapy, as the circumstances became clearer, Katherine began to acknowledge and understand why she had such deep-seated fears in dealing with men. Two adult men in her early life were self-serving and abusive in their own ways. Who wouldn't be afraid to relate to men after these types of experiences?

Now that we have completed these two in-depth case examples of the intrusive parenting style and the distant/hostile parenting style, we are next going to discuss strategies for healing and resolution. We will discuss these strategies first from a psychological perspective and then from a spiritual/metaphysical perspective.

Chapter 9
Psychological Transcendence

Letting go is the lesson.
Letting go is always the lesson.
Have you ever noticed how much of our
agony is all tied up with craving and loss?

Susan Gordon Lydon

At this point, you probably realize that your parent's behavior is more than just commonplace immaturity. You may even have concluded that your parent suffers from a psychological dysfunction that is likely to be a personality disorder. As a result of this awareness, you may also begin to perceive your relationship with your parent in an entirely different light. For example, you may be less likely to normalize or rationalize your parent's behaviors. You may begin to recognize that his or her distressing relationship patterns are related to personality dysfunction. This can be a truly a painful and challenging process, but it also ignites the beginning of psychological awakening.

This chapter is about the tactic of psychological resolution or transcendence through a number of specific psychological strategies. Please keep in mind that inner resolution is a process, not an endpoint. You are not working towards an absolute or *complete* resolution, but rather towards a *relative* resolution. In other words, you may never be "done" dealing with the influence of having had a personality disordered parent, but you can certainly be in a much better place, emotionally, mentally, and spiritually.

Accepting the Presence of Personality Pathology

A psychiatric colleague shared the following story. One busy day on the inpatient psychiatric ward, a medical student was dumbfounded by a patient who was aggressively pulling out her own hair. The medical student approached the supervising psychiatrist and asked, "Why would she do that? Why would she pull out her hair?" The psychiatrist glibly responded, "Because she is a schizophrenic. That's all there is to it." The medical student said nothing more, but remained confused. The patient's behavior just didn't make any sense.

The confusion of the medical student came from relying on logic and a personal frame of reference in an attempt to understand the patient's bizarre behavior. The psychiatrist attempted to emphasize to the student that the patient's behavior was not related to logic. The patient's behavior was due to a psychiatric disorder. Indeed, it is the *lack* of logic that characterizes this form of severe psychiatric disorder. People with mental disorders do not behave and respond to the world in the same ways as healthy people. The attending psychiatrist advised the medical student to stop looking for a rational explanation for the patient's destructive behavior, because there simply wasn't one.

What does this story have to do with you? Well, your parent may suffer from a psychiatric disorder as well—a personality disorder. The diagnosis "personality disorder" may seem like a cold clinical term—one that doesn't even begin to adequately address the emotional pain caused by this dysfunctional individual. However, at least this term offers a tentative intellectual answer for your understandable confusion about your parent's behavior. The behavior still may not make sense logically, but there is at least a reasonable explanation for it.

As in the example of the hair-pulling schizophrenic, the thoughts and behaviors associated with any psychiatric disorder, including personality disorders, are oftentimes not logical, and may be destructive. We feel the need to emphasize this point—*your parent's negative behaviors are never going to make any logical sense to you*. This is a key concept and is the first step in your psychological recovery. For you to move forward with the transcendence process, it is important to *intellectually* accept the conclusion that your parent likely suffers from meaningful psychiatric pathology. As simple as this request sounds, there may be some barriers to such acceptance.

Barriers to Accepting a Parent's Personality Disorder Diagnosis

A surprising number of individuals resist the idea that their parents have personality pathology. Some find it difficult to believe that their parents, who are seemingly normal or successful in so many ways, harbor a psychiatric disorder. How could a mental disorder lie beneath the surface of such a normal-appearing exterior?

As we discussed before, we believe that personality disorders are particularly perplexing to accept as psychiatric disorders because the affected individuals so often have a well-established and somewhat functional façade. However, this paradox of appearing normal on the outside and being dysfunctional on the inside is entirely consistent with the construct of a personality disorder.

It may be particularly difficult to think of your parent as psychologically disordered if he or she was successful financially. Society measures success in dollars and cents, so it's easy to equate financial accomplishment with overall ability. In reality, financial success is not dependent on psychological health. Look at the numerous wealthy and famous, yet troubled, public figures who regularly fill the pages of the tabloid magazines. If your parent was a successful professional, accept that while the element of professional success adds to your confusion, it does not eliminate the possibility of a personality disorder. Personality disorders show themselves most clearly in the context of close relationships, especially with family.

Another explanation for resisting that a parent has personality pathology is the well-known tendency for victims of trauma to blame themselves at some level, thereby shifting the light of scrutiny from the perpetrator onto oneself. So, being the victim of a pathological parent can predictably cloud one's judgment and result in attributing the cause of parent/child dysfunction to oneself. If this tendency rings true for you, actively challenge it.

Accepting that your parent has personality pathology may result in feeling a unique kind of loss. "No matter what he/she was like at home, he/she was *my* parent." It may feel as if acknowledging the presence of a personality disorder takes away the parent's value, or the important role he/she played in your life. However, this is clearly not the case. An individual with a personality disorder is more than just the features that make up that disorder, and there were likely positive aspects to enjoy and characteristics to be proud of. Accepting that your parent has a personality disorder does not mean that everything about him/her is negative or harmful.

Some individuals are resistant to accepting the idea of parental personality pathology because of fear—fear that if the parent genuinely harbors personality pathology, it may be passed on in one way or another. In reality, if you are reaching out for personal growth, it's unlikely that you suffer from a personality disorder (recall that personality disordered individuals rarely have insight into their own dysfunction so they rarely seek psychological help). The fact that you are reading this book is indicative of healthier functioning. Be glad.

A Practical Exercise

The following exercise may help you more quickly achieve an intellectual awareness of your parent's personality disorder. For the moment, take the focus off *your* relationship with your personality disordered parent. Instead, objectively examine your parent's behavior in the context of other family relationships. If you were an outsider peering in, what would you see? We're guessing that in your parent's relationships with others, you might see the same pathological behaviors you experienced in your relationship with your parent (perhaps to a more or less subtle degree).

As an adult, it is now important for you to peer through the veils of despair, anger, guilt, and denial, and to acknowledge the truth. The truth may be that your parent suffers from a personality disorder, and that this type of psychopathology explains the paradoxes observed in your parent. This premise needs to be accepted without any blame and with extreme emotional neutrality—as a simple fact, not a moral judgment. Learn to accept and make peace with your parent's probable psychiatric malady.

Depersonalize the Experience

It is fully understandable that you, as the child, would envision your role in the parent-child interaction as vital, real, relevant, and important. In this way, you are able to retain the illusion of having some unique meaning to your parent and a sense of control with regard to the parent-child relationship ("I *am* a part of this equation!"). You may have even felt and believed at times that you had a direct impact on your parent and could make genuine changes in this dysfunctional relationship. In other words, you may believe that you had such a powerful influence in the parent/child relationship that you caused your parent to act a certain way, at least at times. So, you may believe that you caused your parent to scream, break things, and strike out at others. You may even believe that you caused him or her to administer extreme punishment. When these beliefs are present, there is usually a sense of guilt and remorse over numerous childhood experiences.

Now, think this through carefully. In objective terms, how can a child possibly coerce an adult into acting a particular way? What kind of real interpersonal power resides within a child? Spend some time thinking about this and allow for a new, more realistic perspective. *How the dysfunctional adult reacted to you was due to his or her personality disorder*. In turn, the personality disorder was a product of his or her own genetic makeup, childhood history, and personal traumas. At some point, these contributing factors became hard-wired into your parent's personality—years ago, well before you were conceived. So, accept that your true relevance in the parent/child relationship was likely minimal. This realization has the potential to be painful, or at least disappointing, yet it also can be extremely freeing as well.

Keep in mind that personality disordered parents typically do not respond to situations based on the unique characteristics of those situations. They don't have that kind of behavioral repertoire or flexibility. They tend to react in a stereotypical fashion, with predictable and reactionary behaviors that are usually unconscious and automatic. These "auto-pilot" behaviors have been well solidified over the years. Therefore, it is important for you to realize that, while the interaction between you and your parent seemed very personal, unique, and "in the moment," it probably was not really experienced that way by your parent.

In most cases, another person could have been substituted for you and placed in the same relationship with your parent, and you would have observed the same parental response. We suspect this is a difficult concept to accept. So, ask yourself, "Would my personality disordered parent really have been able to raise anyone else any better? Would I really want my parent raising my child?"

In summary, the ways in which your personality disordered parent responded to you were more likely a reflection of his or her underlying pathology rather than a genuinely unique response to the current and novel situations you presented. So, it seems practical to begin to recognize and acknowledge your *minimal* role in the dysfunctional interactions with your parent, no matter how much your parent attempted to attribute his or her behavior to you ("You made me do that!"). Embrace this new psychological perspective. You no longer need to consciously or unconsciously personalize your parent's behavior. Doing so only creates inner psychological tension for you without helping to accurately understand this perplexing relationship. Embrace reality. Excuse yourself.

Detach from the Idea of the Perfect Parent

Oftentimes, when individuals are first intellectually embracing the fact that their parent has a personality disorder, there is a second and perhaps more subtle underlying mirage to address—the fantasy parent. Sometimes having a *bad* parent compels the adult child to fantasize about what having a *good* parent would be like by contrast. These musings and daydreams may result in the fantasy construction of a perfect parent. A parent who is always there for you. A parent who unconditionally loves, appreciates, values, validates, supports, and mentors you. A parent who you can always talk to and trust. A parent on whom you can always rely.

Wishing for all these qualities in a parent is understandable and quite normal. However, to sustain an unrealistic preoccupation with the fantasy parent is to remain stuck. Continuing to fantasize about illusory perfect parents isn't likely to help you deal more effectively with your own life now that you're an adult. It is important to remove this roadblock to growth by realizing and relinquishing these fantasies. It's not so difficult when we begin to think about other fantasies we've had to relinquish. For example, we had to relinquish the fantasy that everything would be perfect once we got a driver's license, a college degree, a first apartment, or a romantic relationship. (And what about Santa Claus and the Tooth Fairy?) While these events and characters surely made circumstances better for you at the time, they didn't create the perfect life. So, let go of the perfect-parent fantasy, no matter how remote in your consciousness this fantasy seems to be.

Resolve Your Own Anger

Harboring anger towards a personality disordered parent is fully understandable and justified. There is absolutely no need to apologize for, or feel guilty about, such anger. It's a natural and human response to such a detrimental set of experiences. You developed in an unhealthy family situation and it wasn't fair. There need be no doubt about the unjustness of this situation. So, accept your anger as fully legitimate. Acknowledge and validate your anger as completely reasonable.

Given that your anger is legitimate, recognize that this emotion is ultimately a two-edged sword. While one side of the blade is emotionally justifiable anger (you are entitled to your anger based upon your realistic negative life experiences), the other side of the blade is emotional entanglement. You may not realize it, but your anger keeps you *entangled* in your painful experiences. Appreciate that anger can only be emotionally activated through recollections—reliving or re-experiencing past events. Re-experiencing is a form of re-traumatization. Therefore, through your anger, you remain a continual observer to the injustices that were heaped upon you as a child. It's like playing in your head a horrific news clip again and again, as the media often does immediately after a tragedy.

In addition to re-traumatization through recollection, your anger functions as an unconscious emotional connection to the perpetrator. In healthy relationships, we typically think of the emotional "glue" or connection in a positive sense, through feelings of love, admiration, respect, and trust. However, in this alternative scenario involving a negative connection, anger is the emotional glue. This over-powering emotion is unintentionally functioning to connect you to your personality disordered parent. In other words, your anger unintentionally fuels in your mind an ongoing and intense emotional presence or connection with the perpetrator, and functions as a kind of glue that steadfastly bonds you, the victim, with your parent. The result is a trauma bond—an unnatural, illogical, but intense emotional bond that develops under adverse circumstances.

Viewed from another perspective, recognize that anger is not a means to psychologically distance someone. Rather, anger psychologically draws you closer—especially anger that is seemingly justified. It entangles you in the situation. While you are reviewing past legitimate injustices, the perpetrator is very present and very close—in your thoughts and in your mind. Granted, this process is occurring on a totally unconscious level, but it is occurring. Therefore, it is critical for you to begin to work towards neutralizing your anger (which is easier said than done).

In challenging this emotion, you might pose yourself with the following proposition. Do you want to stay angry and enmeshed with your personality disordered parent? Or do you want to make a positive move toward psychological empowerment and freedom? By releasing your anger, you are freeing yourself of longstanding and negative emotional debris. You are also being open to the world around you by *not* being preoccupied and distracted with your past negative experiences and injustices. Finally, you are freeing yourself of the physical and emotional tension that accompanies the re-experiencing of these painful recollections—recollections that fuel your anger. Simply put, relinquishing anger is emotionally good for you.

Resistance to Relinquishing Anger

What's getting in the way of relinquishing your anger? A common response involves the concern that letting go of one's anger is a form of forgiveness. By no longer being angry, the perpetrator is somehow absolved of wrongdoing.

Conversely, by keeping the anger active, the individual's "crimes" are never forgotten or trivialized. In this way, anger acknowledges and sustains a permanent and internal record of injustice. This perspective is fully understandable, but not actually true. Holding on to anger doesn't make the offenses any more or less real. Holding on to anger doesn't make the offenses any more or less forgivable.

Relinquishing your anger has nothing to do with absolving the offender. It's not the equivalent of saying, "I forgive you." It *is* saying, "I am no longer willing to intentionally contaminate my life with negative emotions related to my personality disordered parent. I am no longer willing to stay connected to my personality disordered parent through a trauma bond."

Another possible justification for remaining angry with your parent is that you may be using this intense emotion to maintain a *necessary* emotional connection to him or her. By staying in your own anger, you can unconsciously maintain the parent-child dyad in your head, and thereby protect yourself from *losing* your parent and being alone. Through your anger, your parent is always there—in your thoughts. He or she never leaves you. As bizarre as this may sound, as long as the dysfunctional parent is "present" in one's mind, there is eternal protection against the loss of one's parental figure and what he or she represents. However, once your anger is challenged and relinquished, the personality disordered parent begins to fade and dissipate. That painful chapter of your life is closed.

Some individuals hang onto a dysfunctional relationship with the parent through anger because of the misguided hope of change. "Surely he or she might change at some point!" As one patient poignantly stated, "It's not that I'm in denial— perhaps I just hope a little too much." Recall, however, that personality disorders are enduring and not likely to improve, at least not without considerable personal effort and professional help. You may have to simply accept that your parent, with his or her personality disorder, is all there is.

As a final possibility, you may be resistant to relinquishing your anger because of a general resistance to change how you feel about your parent and your childhood. If so, you may have to challenge yourself and ask: do I really want to move on? Do I *really, really* want to move on? Is the basic roadblock in the transcendence process my own personal resistance to *any* type of change in my feelings? If so, identify the beliefs and assumptions that may underlie your resistance. What is the fear in responding differently to your parent? Why are you stuck?

In summary, if you find yourself hesitant to resolve your anger with your personality disordered parent, explore the reasons why. Do you view the surrendering of your anger as a form of forgiveness? Does letting go of your anger somehow seem to minimize the crimes? Does anger foster a necessary connection to your parent? Are you angry because you unrealistically fantasize that your parent can and might change? Are you resistant to the prospect of change itself in relation to your parent? Whatever the reason, it's time to bring it into the light and carefully examine its logic.

Accept without Condoning

We recognize that perhaps the most difficult goal in this process is to learn to *accept* your parent's behavior without condoning it or approving of it. The key here is neutral acceptance. By this, we mean that it is fundamentally healing to inwardly admit and acknowledge your parent's faulty behavior as a mental dysfunction, but not to feel that your perspective excuses or invalidates the behavior.

Through the process of developing and deepening your awareness, you can begin to acknowledge your parent's destructive behaviors and their potential ramifications in a more rational and *neutral* fashion—again, without excusing them. This is akin to the philosophy, "Reality is what it is, and my feelings about it don't change that reality." Accept that the dysfunction is present, accept that the dysfunction has been destructive to you, and accept that it's not likely to change. Neutral acceptance is emotional resolution—not a sign of weakness, of giving in, or condoning bad behavior.

Consider the "Benefits" of Bad Parenting

Bad parenting is usually perceived by the adult child as an absolutely and completely detrimental experience. It's quite understandable to view the personality disordered parent from this extreme perspective. However, such an all-or-nothing perspective tends to unintentionally promote being stuck psychologically and emotionally. As crazy as it may sound at first, let's consider the possible *benefits* of having had a dysfunctional parent.

Nearly all individuals and relationships can be characterized as unique mixtures of good and bad, and while there may have been a number of unbearable and damaging aspects in your relationship with your personality disordered parent, there surely must have been some positive aspects in the relationship, as well. What was the good? What positive qualities in your parent can you identify and acknowledge? These questions are not intended to excuse bad parenting, but to help ensure not getting caught up in a simplistic, narrow, and unhealthy viewpoint. It's acknowledging the good, the bad, and the ugly (instead of only the bad and the ugly).

In addition to acknowledging your parent's innately good qualities, it is critically important to examine any potential benefits that may have come to you through bad parenting. Sincerely ask yourself, "In what way did this dysfunctional experience propel me in a more positive direction?" As an example, bad parenting sometimes results in offspring who become great parents. When asked, these exceptional parents explain, "I just do the opposite of what my own mother/father did. He/she taught me everything that I *didn't* want to do." Likewise, through adverse interpersonal experiences with your dysfunctional parent, you may have also learned what *not to do* in other relationships and areas of life.

There are numerous examples of possible what-not-to-do benefits. For example, an addicted parent may unintentionally teach a child to avoid alcohol and drugs, without ever having to say so. A physically sloppy parent may propel a child to take exceptional care of his/her body, environment, and/or job. A parent who factually lies may sensitize a child to never engage in lying. A parent with a lack of boundaries may stimulate his or her offspring to be particularly attuned to boundary issues in relationships with others. So, seriously examine the potential for some personal growth that may have unexpectedly emerged from your troubled relationship with your parent. Recognize and appreciate that personal growth. Perhaps without your intense experience with a dysfunctional parent, you would never have received this unexpected "gift."

Strengthen Your Ties with Healthy Others

The only way to become a better tennis player is to play with players who are better than you. This same philosophy applies to developing and improving your relationship skills. As long as you stay enmeshed in a dysfunctional relationship with a parent (or with a dysfunctional partner, dysfunctional friends, or a dysfunctional family), you are unlikely to learn healthier and more sophisticated relationship skills. In other words, when you come from a background of numerous dysfunctional family relationships, it is extremely important to learn about healthy relationships through experiences *outside* of the family. You need to develop and strengthen your relationships with individuals who are emotionally "better players." You need them to stimulate your own growth and develop your own relationship skills.

Misery Loves Company

The preceding suggestion does not mean that you should indiscriminately seek out relationships with others other than your parents. To blindly seek out outside relationships without forethought carries definite risks. For example, we have often noted that the adult children of dysfunctional parents tend to seek out other adult children who have dysfunctional relationships with their parents.

As a consequence, each individual mutually "uses" the new peer relationship to commiserate about and garner support for their experiences with their personality disordered parent. While these types of relationships may be initially satisfying (it's always gratifying to experience validation from someone else who's "been there"), many times they don't really offer genuine opportunities for growth in relationship skills. At their worst, they perpetuate being stuck. So, in developing outside relationships, the idea is to thoughtfully and intentionally engage *healthy* individuals who exhibit the kinds of relationship skills you desire.

An Older Mentor

Some people have found it very beneficial to develop a mentoring relationship with someone who is the same sex and approximate age as their dysfunctional parent. These "adoptive" parents can sometimes accelerate the healing process because of their unique resonance with your emotional needs for a functional parent. We're not saying that this healing role should take the place of genuine friendship as the basis for the relationship. Still, it may be an important side benefit.

As a caveat, realize that enjoying a genuine friendship with someone in your parent's age group may initially highlight the deficits in your own parent, which is a painful experience. "Why couldn't my parent have been more like you?" But again, recognize your parent's deficits on a reality level and accept them as a part of your own personal growth. In the long run, the healing potential of bonding with this type of mentor is immeasurable.

Continuing to Grow

One recurrent dilemma in working with individuals with personality disordered parents is the decision around whether to continue contact with the parent during adulthood. Specifically, should there be *any* contact during adulthood? If so, what type and/or degree of contact? These are legitimate questions that only you can answer. Candidly ask yourself, "Does having contact of any type or degree with my dysfunctional parent significantly impede my growth and/or independence?"

Promoting Differentiation and Individuation

From a psychological perspective, we would rephrase "growth and independence" as, *"differentiation* ("I am not you. I am separate from you.") and *individuation* ("I am my own unique person.")." Differentiation is the recognition that you are not merely a psychological extension of your parent, but a unique and independent individual with your own personality. Individuation is the unfolding of your unique features and characteristics. It is the assimilation of your true identity. Differentiation and individuation are natural and necessary developmental processes that begin shortly after birth and continue throughout the lifespan, but are most recognizable during the first few years of life and again during adolescence. First comes the recognition of separateness and then comes the consolidation of selfhood.

Typically, personality disordered parents establish enmeshed and highly dysfunctional relationships with their children, which dramatically inhibits or impairs the process of differentiation and individuation. These parents do not allow for separateness or an individual identity.

They do not allow for personal growth. Dysfunctional parents *misinterpret* differentiation and individuation as emotional abandonment or betrayal. Therefore, if your current relationship with your parent is highly constricted in this manner, it is probably prudent for you to seriously consider eliminating all contact with your parent (i.e., a "parent-ectomy").

Given the range of possibilities on the continuum of personality disorder, your parent may have only mild to moderate dysfunction. In this case, you may be able to continue a relationship to some degree with your personality disordered parent if the pathology does not realistically impair your ongoing process of differentiation and individuation (i.e., personal growth). Again, only *you* can honestly address this issue for yourself, because you are the only one who truly knows to what degree your parent's dysfunction is a hindrance to your own potential for personal growth.

Assessing Parental Responses to Differentiation

How do you assess parental tolerance of differentiation and individuation? The degree of parental resistance to this process lies along a continuum, which likely reflects the degree of pathology in your parent. In severe cases, dysfunctional parents are keenly aware of and disapproving of *any* attempt by their offspring to differentiate and individuate. They are exquisitely threatened by their child's natural push to establish a personal identity and independence. The highly dysfunctional parent doesn't acknowledge this process as a necessary progression in the human developmental experience, but rather as a sign of impending abandonment or betrayal by the child. In other words, the child's growth and independence are typically misconstrued by the needy parent as psychological desertion and by the narcissistic parent as rebellion or betrayal. And we all know what happens to deserters and betrayers. They have to be executed (in this case, psychologically executed).

In anticipation of the child's push for selfhood, highly dysfunctional parents typically heap on unhealthy dogma around separation and independence. The dominant message to the child and/or young adult is that to grow as an individual is somehow inherently bad (e.g., selfish, inconsiderate, uncaring, dangerous). That self-growth is going to lead to some ominous and tragic outcome for the child. In reality, the reverse is more likely—that the child's growth will result in the collapse of the parent.

Note that this theme of "an inability to survive" is actively projected onto the child by the parent. "It's not that *I* can't survive—it's that *you* can't survive." This philosophy may be communicated to the child on a variety of levels and in a number of different ways, especially on a verbal level. "You might think you're something special, but you can't really make it on your own." "A good child would never abandon his/her mother." "The people out there, they will just hurt you. Mark my words." "You're different. Don't you know that? You won't ever be able to have a successful relationship out there." "Deep down, no one will ever really love you like I do." On occasion, the parental statements are more transparent and may be as startling as, "You can't leave me alone; I will die." "If you leave me, I will kill myself."

Please examine the preceding statements carefully. Most of them are actually projections (i.e., beliefs that the parent holds about himself/herself, but which are unconsciously attributed to or projected onto his/her offspring). These statements function as attempts to keep the child in the dysfunctional family fold through *fear* and *insecurity* (not love and compassion). As a result, deep within the adult child, there may be an unrealistic and unhealthy discomfort about autonomy and independence (i.e., selfhood)—one that has been programmed by the dysfunctional parent to magically keep hold of the child forever.

Unfortunately, many adult children tend to initially *deny* the degree of impediment in their relationship with their personality disordered parents. They may rationalize or minimize the situation in a number of different ways. "It's really not that bad." "I probably exaggerate—Mom isn't the monster that I portray her to be in here." "I am probably just being overly sensitive." "Whose parents aren't crazy?"

Despite these attempts to initially minimize the dysfunction and its personal negative impact, oftentimes the opposite is the case in reality. The parent may be far worse than described, but the patient cannot emotionally acknowledge the depth of this dysfunction. This is because we all have built-in survival mechanisms to get through difficult situations. These adaptive psychological mechanisms function to minimize the badness of a situation. Some examples of these adaptive psychological mechanisms are denial ("It's simply not so"), suppression ("I will shove this unacceptable bit of data into my unconscious"), or even distortion (e.g., "Well, I enjoyed some of it; therefore, it couldn't really be called sexual abuse;" "He only beat me so that I'd learn my lesson!"). These are often the necessary tools that enable a distressed child to psychologically survive a very challenging life with an impaired parent. Therefore, when working with patients, we typically find ourselves on the alert for denial and other defense mechanisms.

Anticipating Resistance to Changing the Relationship

If you initially undertake a middle-of-the-road position and attempt to restructure the parent/adult-child relationship, note how your parent responds. Parents with personality pathology, however minimal, rarely understand the authentic reasons for any "change" in the parent-child relationship. They may feel threatened with *any* restructuring of the relationship and desperately attempt to force the relationship back to its original position. In doing so, they may be argumentative and demeaning ("Why are you doing this to us?"), blame others for your seemingly new attitude ("It's your therapist/new girlfriend/ best friend/spouse who put these notions in your head."), or even threaten you ("If you pull this stunt, you'll be out of the will!").

It's normal to experience a regressive tug back towards "the way it was." Hang tough. When these kinds of responses arise from very minimal forms of differentiation/individuation, it is an ominous sign that the parent is threatened by virtually any degree of autonomy and selfhood. If this is the case, you may need to re-think how realistic it is to form a more moderate relationship with your parent.

Performing a Total Parent-ectomy

In a severely dysfunctional relationship between an adult child and his or her parent, a total parent-ectomy may be necessary. The idea of a parent-ectomy may surprise you. To *totally sever* a relationship with a parent, no matter how dysfunctional or impaired that parent is, may sound unnecessarily and unacceptably cold, indifferent, or uncaring. However, at times, it's critically necessary for one's psychological survival.

Resistance to a parent-ectomy is commonly bolstered by the societal premise that, "Family is family," and "Blood is thicker than water." Ironically, society seems to support leaving a destructive relationship with a drug-addicted and physically abusive romantic partner. In fact, to stay in such a dysfunctional and self-defeating relationship might be seen as "crazy." But what's the actual difference between a disturbed and destructive relationship with a partner versus a disturbed and destructive relationship with a parent?

In addition to seeing the termination of a relationship with one's parent as cold and indifferent, society may see such a termination as having taken the "easy way out." "You just need to work harder at this relationship." In response, we emphasize that it takes a great deal of courage and determination to terminate an unhealthy relationship with personality disordered parents. They are the only parents that you have ever known, and you have known them your entire life. Therefore, to successfully disengage from these intensely sticky relationships takes a great deal of emotional energy, strength, and fortitude. Rather than being the "easy way out," we think that it's just the opposite—that it's a very difficult and *courageous* path, not to be undertaken lightly.

Accept the Co-Parent's Responsibility for the Family Situation

The dysfunctional parent is the standout—he or she is the self-centered, manipulative, controlling, and offensive one. Quite frankly, this parent seems rather obvious in the panoramic backdrop of the home environment. However, there is oftentimes a second parent in the home, the co-parent. The co-parent is typically participating in, allowing, and/or denying the partner's pathology. The co-parent may not seem *overtly* harmful, yet may be *covertly* harmful through his or her relatively more passive role in the family tragedy.

While the personality disordered parent has been seen as the villain, the co-parent may be unrealistically viewed as the "good parent." Perhaps the co-parent may have even functioned as an illusory safety net or protector for the children. In some cases, adult children may even believe that the co-parent was the *only* thing that got them through their early years of chaotic home life. On occasion, the co-parent may even attain a kind of savior-like status.

So, it may be difficult to recognize that the co-parent *may* have played a role in the maintenance of your family's dysfunction. It's possible that you see this assertion as heresy. Indeed, you may feel that, by raising this possibility, we are attacking the "good" parent. However, it is critically important to identify the co-parent's actual role in this dysfunctional situation. A full understanding of the family dynamics, and of both parents' roles in it, is necessary to experience truth. And, this includes a realistic view of the co-parent.

Not all co-parents are, themselves, dysfunctional. However, people frequently choose life partners who fill roles complementary to their own role. Therefore, there is the very strong possibility that one type of personality pathology resonates with a different type of personality pathology.

As an example of co-parent dynamics, a patient described how her hardworking mother had married an abusive, unemployed alcoholic. As a result, her mother had to work long hours at several jobs to support him and her family of three children. She had few skills and began cleaning houses. The patient always admired her mother's fortitude and believed that her mother had *saved* the family, despite a highly dysfunctional stepfather.

However, when we examine this vignette more closely, some interesting questions emerge. First, why did the mother *stay* married to an unemployed alcoholic? Granted, she might not have recognized her mistake early on, but after years of his monetary and emotional non-contribution, why stay with him? Second, why didn't the mother seek out a partner in life who was willing and able to participate as an adult in an adult-to-adult relationship? Third, and most concerning, why would she expose her children to an active and abusive alcoholic?

So, in this case, it *is* admirable that the patient's mother supported her family. However, it's also very concerning that she made such very poor decisions for her family—specifically, marrying and remaining with an unsupportive and hostile alcoholic. Interestingly, one of this patient's siblings held this latter view. She was appropriately very angry at her mother for having made such a bad marital choice—a choice that lasted for years and deeply affected all of the children.

Address the Attitudes of Your Siblings

Your siblings experienced each parent in a slightly different way than you did. As such, they have their own interpretations of the various family members and childhood experiences, and these may not match yours. Even if they agree that things were difficult, they may not share the same solution (e.g., a full parent-ectomy). Siblings tend to either value emotional growth and differentiation/individuation or they espouse the philosophy of "family togetherness at all costs."

It is essential to consider your relationship with each sibling on its own merit. Has your sibling experienced substantial damage? Does the relationship with your sibling promote in you a sense of personal validation and growth? Or, does the relationship with your sibling keep you stuck in old family patterns? Only you can determine whether each sibling relationship is an overall asset or liability.

Unfortunately, there may come a time when you realize that some or all of your siblings have highly dysfunctional tendencies. This outcome is more likely with more toxic parenting. In these cases, you may have to face the sad possibility of *relinquishing* your relationships with siblings, particularly if they continue to play out toxic roles and dysfunctional behaviors. We realize this is difficult to consider; it's a difficult thing for us to have to say. However, the point of the life experience is growth and understanding, not being battered by your emotionally dysfunctional siblings. Your psychological and emotional health is the key point of this consideration.

Accept the Possible Absence of Blood Family

At times, entire family systems are extremely dysfunctional. In these circumstances, people often worry that if they disengaged from all of their dysfunctional and unhealthy family relationships, they would have no one. It is true—if you have to take this drastic measure, you will have no relationships with the majority of your genetic family members. While this proposition may sound a bit overwhelming, it may be necessary if a number of your family members suffer from severe impairment due to personality pathology. When they do, you may be forced to make a choice—be free and perhaps relatively alone, or be emotionally incarcerated and surrounded by a host of individuals with damaging and severe psychopathology.

It is truly difficult, and sometimes terrifying, to entertain the prospect of "going it alone" in life. Unfortunately, that's what dysfunctional parents and family members are counting on—that you will be too afraid to disengage from them. They may even feed such fears by undermining your confidence and making your decisions seem unchangeable. "You can't make it on your own, out there." "If you walk through that door, don't plan on coming back." "*You* are the problem."

However, realize that as long as you are tied up in these dysfunctional relationships, there is no remaining emotional energy to develop alternative and healthier relationships. Unfortunately, you may have to first truly and fully disengage from these dysfunctional relationships before re-attaching to others who are healthier.

This process reminds us of a recent experience shared by a patient. He was very hesitant to discard a pair of black sandals, which were clearly worn out. He responded that he was afraid that he wouldn't be able to find any suitable replacements. His wife promptly confronted him and said, "You won't look for any new sandals until you've thrown out the old ones." He reluctantly disposed of the sandals and began to look for replacements. To his surprise, he promptly found a pair of black sandals that were much better.

On a cautionary note, in some cases, individuals with dysfunctional families will attempt to establish a transitional relationship (e.g., boyfriend, girlfriend) before leaving the family unit. This is usually an unconscious attempt to pre-establish a safety net prior to a risky emotional departure from the family. However, because the motive for this type of relationship is as an exit strategy, it's unlikely that there will be the firm foundation for a healthy, long-term relationship. When the escape from the dysfunctional family is complete, the cracks in the foundation often become more apparent.

While exodus from the family may initially seem like a terrifying concept, our clinical experience indicates that re-attachment to others is quite likely. So, while the fear of being alone is very understandable, it does not appear to actually materialize very often. Rest assured that initiating the process of emotional emancipation is very likely to allow for healthier relationships and better interpersonal connections with others. Conversely, being emotionally trapped in an enmeshed and dysfunctional family must feel very much like being in prison—isolating, lonely, and stifling. The choice is yours.

Chapter 10
Spiritual Transcendence

The problem is that we tend to seek...
easy and painless answers.
But this kind of solution does
not apply to the spiritual path.
Chogyam Trungpa Rinpoche

From the outset, dealing with a personality disordered parent must seem like an onerous and never-ending burden. Our parents affect our lives from the very beginning, and that effect has insidious and profound consequences on our unfolding self-concepts and our relationships with others. Unfortunately, the personality disordered parent tends to generate continual adversity and stress for everyone in the household, including his or her own offspring. As a result, the personality disordered parent could be summed up as a genuine obstacle in the overall course of one's life.

Obstacles: Western & Eastern Perspectives

What is an obstacle? Two distinct perspectives—Western and Eastern—indicate that the answer is not absolute. From a Western viewpoint, an obstacle is traditionally defined as an impediment—something that gets in the way or blocks one from a goal. The Western connotation of the word *obstacle* is clearly negative and the emphasis is on avoiding obstacles when possible, and overcoming them when not.

From an Eastern perspective, obstacles are viewed as opportunities for growth. Obstacles are seen as temporary impasses in the life experience and have the potential to foster significant internal growth through the process of resolution. They are not to be avoided or resisted, but embraced and worked through when encountered.

Consider two hypothetical people, each of whom holds the goal of financial security. Suppose the first person comes from a very wealthy family. However, the portion of family wealth left to this particular person comes with a stipulation: she must earn a college degree before receiving her inheritance (which, by the way, is large enough that she'll never need to work a day in her life). In contrast, the second person decides that, to have the career she wants, she needs to earn a college degree.

Will the two hypothetical women view the college experience differently? Probably very differently. The first woman is liable to see college as an obstacle between her and the assurance of financial independence. For her, a college degree is something to be overcome along her life's journey. The second is liable to see college as a stepping stone to where she wants to be—the path she needs to get there. Both women will likely earn a degree, but which is most likely to benefit from the process? Who is more liable to grow personally as a result of earning that degree?

Now, what about your personality disordered parent? Challenge yourself to reframe your dysfunctional parent's purpose in your life and no longer view him or her as a disruption along your life's path. On the contrary, envision that parent as a unique challenge that will ultimately lead to vital personal growth. In other words, the obstacle will likely unfold for a higher purpose.

Have you heard of the famous Biosphere—the enclosed, self-sufficient, man-made environment in Arizona? One difficulty that the researchers encountered in this scientifically created world was that the trees would only grow to a particular height and then would fall over. As puzzling as this phenomenon was initially, the researchers ultimately discovered that the lack of wind inside the dome resulted in shallow root growth. Without sufficiently deep roots, the trees simply fell over when they reached a height that could no longer be supported by the shallow roots.

Wind is necessary for the dispersion of strong tree roots and the ultimate stabilization of the tree. Similarly, obstacles are necessary for the deepening growth and stabilization of the psychological self and the spiritual self. So, rather than perceiving obstacles as frustrating impediments, we must begin to reframe them as part of the natural course of life and as essential to growth. When confronted by a frustrated student who complained of continued obstacles in his path, a Zen master replied, "the obstacle *is* the path."

Just a Coincidence?

Another spiritual theme to consider with regard to your personality disordered parent is whether your life's unfolding is simply coincidental. Specifically, is your parent/obstacle a random event or was this relationship somehow intended for you, as a unique being? In other words, is there some greater design for your spiritual growth and unfolding? Regardless of your religious or spiritual orientation, there are some important psychological advantages to embracing the intriguing philosophy that there are no coincidences. Let's examine the potentially positive implications of this philosophy.

Advantages to the "No-Coincidences" Philosophy

First, if there are no coincidences, then it follows that everything is as it should be. Simply put, regardless of how it appears to you, everything is in its place. If you have a personality disordered parent, then it is no coincidence. There must be some deeper, necessary spiritual function that this relationship serves. One of the most common "benefits" of these detrimental relationships is teaching us what *not* to do in life. Indeed, from a spiritual perspective, perhaps all negative life events and dysfunctional people serve as dramatic guideposts for the rest of us—functioning as reminders of what we are *not* to do. So, like other forms of adversity, perhaps personality disordered parents serve the same purposeful function.

Second, if there truly are no coincidences, then the fundamental task becomes embracing and exploring your relationship with a dysfunctional parent in the service of personal growth and maturation (instead of trying to figure out why your parent is the way he or she is). Rather than needing to understand the dysfunctional parent, the task becomes more exterior, functional, and unilateral in nature. "Regardless of why my parent is this way, how is it supposed to *benefit* me?" From this perspective, your parent and your relationship are examined in ways that result in psychological and spiritual momentum for you—a process that promotes self and spiritual maturation.

Third, if there are no coincidences, then getting caught up in negative emotions about being challenged with this type of obstacle is unnecessary and wasteful. The obstacle is here as a reference point for growth. Getting stuck in resisting the obstacle results in the unnecessary squandering of your emotional resources. Rather than struggling against the presence of the obstacle, the task for you is to emotionally surrender to its presence and examine the obstacle from a broader growth perspective. Again, what is its purpose? In what ways are you supposed to grow from your experiences with a dysfunctional parent?

If you believe in reincarnation, then you likely believe you have specific tasks to achieve during each lifetime. How might these tasks be uniquely tied to this specific obstacle in this lifetime? If you do not believe in reincarnation, but accept that there are no coincidences, why might you have been tasked with this particular obstacle? From an existential perspective, what are you supposed to achieve in terms of self-development through struggling with and resolving this challenging task?

In summary, when reflecting about the obstacles in your life, you have the option of entertaining two basic perspectives—a randomness perspective or a no-coincidences perspective. Psychologically, we believe that the *no coincidences* philosophy fosters much better mental health. We don't expect you to agree, just yet. So, let's further examine the cognitive and emotional processes associated with these two perspectives— randomness versus no-coincidences—to clarify the advantages of one over the other.

Take Your Pick: Randomness vs. No-Coincidences

If you believe that the obstacles in life are random, you're likely to be resentful of them. "I got screwed." "I don't deserve this." If all of this is random, then being saddled with an obstacle is likely to engender feelings of victimization and hopelessness. "This random obstacle has been placed in my path, and not on the paths of others. That's unfair. I am being victimized and there is nothing that I can do about it."

In contrast, if the obstacle is *not* perceived as random and is actually viewed as serving some greater purpose, then it takes on an entirely different meaning. Given that there is some higher and necessary purpose in dealing with the obstacle, you are now posed with a challenge that is specifically designed for you and your personal growth. Your response might include curiosity, acceptance, and certainly much less fear and anger. As a result, you are likely to develop strategies for responding to rather than reacting to the obstacle. In other words, rather than reacting defensively, you are now more likely to respond creatively, or at least thoughtfully. We believe that better mental health is associated with this approach.

In comparing these two approaches, note that the randomness perspective is liable to leave you feeling demoralized, victimized, and emotionally charged in negative ways, whereas the no-coincidences perspective establishes your role as a psychological sleuth, with your task being to figure out the puzzle (the obstacle) and why it was meant for you.

Seeking Purpose in the Obstacle

Why you, and why this particular personality disordered parent? What is the special skill or response or strategy that you are supposed to recognize and develop from such an obstacle? This level of contemplation is very personal, and requires time for serious thought. In the case of personality disordered parents, you must detach yourself from the surface-level drama—from the dysfunction—and begin to see deeper into the healthy directions you are supposed to go with these experiences. It's an entirely different way of processing the experience. What path is this situation pointing you to?

Presence

Being present means relinquishing "mind-time" spent in the past or spent in the future and existing in the very presence of this moment—in the now. It sounds easy, but we humans tend to spend a great deal of time thinking about the past. For example, when we have experienced a personality disordered parent, we may spend a substantial portion of our mental time and energy sorting through our past horrific experiences and recounting the injustices that were done to us. Each infraction is likely to be pulled out, reviewed, judged, and then meticulously re-encoded into memory so as not to be forgotten. Recognize that this level of focus on the past promotes a kind of "stuckness." There is no way to change the past, no matter how many times we replay the events. On the contrary, as we discussed before, this type of past-focus replay is usually accompanied by re-traumatization (the re-experiencing of traumatic events with the personality disordered parent) and leads to negative feelings such as depression and anger.

We humans also fantasize or worry about the future and what it might bring. Perhaps a healing relationship. Perhaps a chance to be a better parent.

Perhaps a chance to be a better grandparent. Perhaps loss. Perhaps infirmity. Perhaps aloneness. Some individuals even dwell on the future as a habitual way to avoid experiencing the troublesome circumstances of the present. In other words, they may mentally anchor to the future, when things might be better, to avoid experiencing the pain of the present moment. Regardless of some positive benefits, future-focused thinking is usually fear-related and frequently accompanied by anxiety and apprehension. "What if things don't turn out that way? What if this or that goes wrong?"

When you are focusing on the future, you are, again, not being present. You are missing the active essence of the immediate life experience. This narrow space in time is the only reality that you can and ever will genuinely experience as it actually unfolds (in "real" time). This is where your being truly exists—not in the anxiety-laden anticipatory musings of the future. The present is where your genuine emotional satisfaction ultimately resides. Choose the present.

Presence is about anchoring in the here-and-now, and staying there. Choosing presence challenges you to relinquish your preoccupation with the gloomy recollections of the past and the "what-if's" of the future. By staying in the past or future in your head, you are missing what is happening before your very eyes. You are missing the joys (and yes, sadness and every other emotion) of life as people were meant to experience it. Of course this is easier said than done. Living in the present requires practice—specifically the practice of mindfulness.

Mindfulness

The principle of presence seamlessly melds into the principle of mindfulness: *being aware in this very moment*. Mindfulness requires being present in the immediate now and having experiences as they unfold. Therefore, mindfulness is a fundamental key to being and remaining present.

In psychology, the term *selective inattention* refers to an over-focus on an item in the foreground to the exclusion of the context or the background. In other words, a person focuses too much on one object, thereby missing everything else around it. This principle is captured by the old adage "not being able to see the forest for the trees."

This process may account for our tendency as humans to tune in to particular stimuli at the expense of experiencing our broader world in all of its complexity and richness. By staying focused on a specific stimulus (in this case, a dysfunctional parent), we risk sacrificing our broader life experiences, and all their shades of complexity and richness of depth. But what's the alternative?

We encourage the active practice of mindfulness. How? By intentionally focusing on your immediate environment, you become more mindful of life. Take multiple pauses throughout the day, unplug from activity and internal self-talk, and become aware of your sensory experiences. What are the sights, tastes, smells, and sounds of your immediate environment? How does your body feel as it comes into contact with everything else around it? As you do this, stay focused on these experiences, resisting the tendency for your mind to wander away from your awareness of the present. Stay present.

Does the following sound familiar? While driving a habitual route, you find yourself drifting into a "road hypnosis," lost in your thoughts about the past or the tasks that lie ahead. You suddenly realize that you're close to reaching your destination, but can't really account for the driving time, because you haven't been at all present in your experience. You missed most of the experience of the drive because you were entirely in your head.

Your assignment now is to try to use driving as a cue to focus on your surroundings. View them as if you had always been blind, and suddenly gained the ability to see. Really see the shapes and colors; watch all of the movement going on around you. Go beyond the sense of sight. Smell the air. Feel the steering wheel in your hands and the seat against your body. Be present in the vehicle.

When fully present, it's a small step to appreciate that there will never be another moment of experience exactly like this one. Never. Some may be similar, but never exactly the same. This awareness exercise lends itself well to experiences in nature, such as walking or sitting in the woods, in a community park, or near water. Each setting represents an entirely unique experience to appreciate.

Now, consider eating. How often do you eat without really experiencing your food? Sure, you ingest the food and feel full, but have you really spent much time experiencing the food? Feeling its texture? Savoring its taste? Contemplating its smell? One famous Vietnamese monk describes well the principle of mindfulness during mealtimes with his fellow monks. They eat in total silence, not to foster a sense of isolation or lofty being, but rather to be present with the very essence of the food, and thereby experience it.

How does all of this relate to personality disordered parents? Consider the following example. A patient was on the telephone with her highly dysfunctional mother. The mother was intoxicated with prescription analgesics, which was typical for her. The patient broached the issue of a babysitter who molested her and her sister for an entire year during their childhoods. At the time, both girls told their mother about the molestation by the female sitter, but the mother continued to employ the sitter anyway. During the telephone conversation, the mother defensively stated in a slurred voice, "She only molested you girls for a few weeks," as if this nullified the injustice. Understandably, the patient exploded and proceeded to call her mother a number of obscenities.

What happened here? The patient understandably got caught up in the past and her experienced injustices. This dysfunctional mother couldn't possibly validate her distressed daughter in the present—she never had and it was unrealistic to expect that the mother had grown. The daughter was seeking validation in the now, which she so desperately wanted from her mother. Unfortunately, it simply wasn't going to happen. In this painful situation, being present is really about realizing how impaired this mother is, that there will never be any validation from her, and that this level of impairment reflects the severity of the mother's personality disorder.

In describing this example, we sincerely do not mean to minimize the pain of molestation. However, continuing to react to these past traumatic situations as if resolution could occur through re-experiencing the past is not a means towards growth. The molestation happened. It is and was painful. No re-experiencing of the past is ever going to resolve it. It is important to begin to alter your thinking around these types of horrific obstacles and stop re-running the same mental program, which only leads to pain and suffering. In the preceding example, the daughter must retrain herself to look away from the surface content (the molestation) and begin to fully embrace the depth of the moment (the lack of validation from mother)—as bad as it is.

Meditation

Meditation is an invaluable Eastern practice that serves many purposes. For most, meditation is practiced to achieve a deep state of relaxation and to relieve stress. Meditation may also be used to undertake auto-suggestion, or a kind of self-hypnosis. In this regard, because the process creates a very porous and relaxed mind state, the practitioner is more amenable to suggestion during meditation, which can be used to tackle specific problems.

For some, meditation facilitates an extraordinary spiritual experience as a portal to a new psychological dimension—a loftier level of consciousness and being. Finally, meditation has been shown to facilitate an overall sense of momentary well-being through the generation of alpha waves in the brain. It is this latter feature that is so essential for individuals in states of emotional disruption and unhappiness.

Preparing for Meditation

Most meditation experts recommend a quiet, peaceful location, a comfortable sitting position with one's back straight and/or supported, loose comfortable clothing, and a setting in which you are not likely to be disturbed. Eyes are usually partially or fully closed. Most forms of meditation begin by focusing on the breath or breathing. From this point onward, various techniques and variations are possible. In some forms of meditation, there is a focused mantra while other forms center on observing the various thoughts that appear in the mind. However, for our purposes, the following meditation technique is specifically designed for quickly achieving a sense of well-being.

A Simple Meditation Exercise for Well-Being

Begin this meditation experience by closing your eyes and concentrating on your breathing. Really center on your breathing patterns. Hear and feel each breath as it enters your body, fills your lungs, and then leaves your body. As you do this, slowly breathe in, and then slowly breathe out. Slowly breathe in, and then slowly breathe out. Concentrate on this slow, rhythmic pattern until you feel yourself beginning to relax. As you do, allow your breaths to occur naturally. Simply pay attention to your breathing, but do not consciously control it.

While focusing on your breathing, allow yourself to mentally drift into the emerging pattern of physical monotony. Gently clear your mind of any thoughts other than breathing in and breathing out. Then, after several moments, use the following technique, which is employed by some Vietnamese monks. Begin to pair your breathing with the words, "calming" and "smiling." Pair "calming" with each inhalation, and pair "smiling" with each exhalation. As you do this for several minutes, allow yourself to drift into the rhythm of the process. Enjoy the peaceful regularity of the experience. Be very aware of the thoughts that enter your mind. As they emerge, gently and passively allow them to dissipate or fade into nothingness. As they dissipate, return to and focus on your breathing, repeating in your mind, "calming/smiling."

Finally, as you reach a peaceful and porous calm, which generally takes a few minutes after the onset of your meditation practice, shift from "calming/smiling" to focusing on the space between your ears. As an alternative, you can focus on the space between your eyes. This specific focus on space will facilitate the experience of no-mind (i.e., no thinking or no active thoughts). Center here for several minutes, then conclude your meditation experience by slowly and gently returning to your usual state of awareness.

The Alpha Wave Experience

In the preceding exercise, the focus on the *space* between the eyes may sound a bit odd, but it is a critical ingredient in this particular meditation approach. Rather than focusing on an object or image, which promotes the generation of beta waves in the brain, focusing on empty space promotes the rapid and spontaneous generation of alpha waves in the brain. Alpha waves are traditionally associated with an enhanced sense of well-being and are much more dominant in experienced meditators. You should experience this pleasant sensation quickly during the preceding meditation exercise.

Meditation Pointers

The good news is that you don't have to spend an excessive amount of time engaging in meditation to reap the benefits. You can briefly meditate while sitting in your office, in a parking lot (e.g., waiting for a companion to finish errands), or on your sofa. However, spend about 10 minutes or more each day to continue to improve your technique. Like any skill, it gets easier and better with practice. It usually requires sustained practice to learn to overcome mind drift (i.e., thinking about other things, or being distracted by background noises).

After you master this simple meditation induction, you can augment it with auto-suggestion, which is particularly effective in this heightened state of awareness. For example, you may want to suggest to yourself that, "Everything will be fine" (i.e., a phrase to counter or reduce anxiety). Time the words with your breathing. For example, "everything" can be timed with an inhalation, and "will be fine" can be timed with an exhalation.

You can suggest other things to yourself. For example, you may want to promote inner calm (e.g., "I am at peace"). You may want to suggest relinquishing the past (e.g., "Surrender is the key" or "It is what it is"). You may want to focus on developing more mindful eating in an effort to lose weight (e.g., "I experience the food"). The possibilities are endless. Regardless of the phrase, continue to pair your words with your breathing.

Gratitude

We want to be very respectful as we execute the next philosophy—the practice of gratitude. We appreciate that your painful experiences have left you feeling betrayed by life. What on earth is there to be grateful for? Indeed, you may firmly believe that, "I have been shortchanged—it could have been so much better." This is a completely normal response to extreme adversity—feeling persecuted, overwhelmed, and emotionally numb. So, we understand from a humanistic perspective that you may understandably wonder what there is to be grateful about. In reality, however, there are a *number* of things to be genuinely grateful for.

Things to be Grateful For

What might you be grateful for? Think broadly. For example, there is an unprecedented supply and variety of foods that you can eat, and you can enjoy them throughout the year, regardless of the climate. Most of us have warm homes that protect us from the whims of the weather. We are generally safe in our environment. You may have a spouse, partner, friend, or a faithful pet that you deeply appreciate. The point is, you very likely have some very significant people or things to be grateful for. We think it's important to regularly acknowledge these good things and to actively value them. Why?

The Benefits of Gratitude

Why experience and express gratitude? The answer is amazingly simple. Experiencing gratitude appears to promote a general sense of well-being. This amazing benefit has been scientifically highlighted in numerous psychological studies. The following is just one example.

Researchers split a sample of college students into two groups, each of which were asked to keep a daily journal. One group was instructed to journal about the things that they were genuinely grateful for, whereas the other about whatever topic they chose. At the end of the study, the researchers assessed the participants' overall sense of well-being. Not surprisingly, the students who kept a journal of gratitude experienced a significantly greater sense of overall emotional well-being compared to those students who journaled on the topics of their choice.

Given that you had a traumatic parental experience, it is particularly important that you capitalize upon gratefulness. Such experiences may offset or neutralize the negative experiences in your life. Again, positive experiences do exist in all of our lives; unfortunately, we tend to take them for granted. The first step toward gratitude is recognizing the positive aspects of your life. Then allow yourself the pleasure of experiencing the gift.

Gratitude Exercises

Your practice of gratitude may benefit from some practical exercises. One approach is to mimic the journaling experiment developed by the researchers described earlier. That is, keep a journal at your bedside, and before going to bed each night, briefly write down the things in your life that you are grateful for—either for that day, in the recent past, or even in the remote past. Alternatively, do the same when getting up in the morning.

Another very simple gratitude exercise pertains to food. In this exercise, you literally express your gratefulness to the food for being available to you.

Rather than a traditional prayer prior to eating, actively and earnestly thank each source of food for being present on the table. It may sound peculiar at first, but before eating, you might say, "Thank you cows for the milk; thank you wheat for the bread; thank you chicken for the meat; thank you potatoes and corn." It's simplistic, forthright, and concrete. It's an excellent way to foster an ongoing and earnest sense of gratitude.

Importantly, like any habit, gratitude takes practice. So, select a gratitude format and begin to perform it on a regular basis. The practice of gratitude will re-focus your daily thinking toward pleasant experiences and make you feel better emotionally.

Evolutionary Impediments to Gratitude

As biological beings, we are hardwired to keenly encode and remember fearful and/or predatory experiences. To quickly appreciate this concept, think of yourself as a primate on the savannah, with leopards prowling through the high grasses. Then imagine the experience of seeing a friend devoured by a leopard. As horrific as this might be, for this experience to have any survival value, it must be keenly and firmly encoded into your memory—intellectually, visually, and emotionally. So, from an evolutionary perspective, the recollection of trauma serves as a protective reminder to avoid particular places and animals that are dangerous. In other words, the ongoing recollection of trauma guides you to ensure your future survival.

Given this understanding of human hardwiring, the evolutionary drive is naturally to focus on the *negative*, or the traumatic—again, because of its potential survival value. Such biological priming makes the active pursuit of gratitude all the more important. Your brain is going to naturally gravitate towards focusing on negative experiences, thus drawing you back into excessive head time with the traumatic recollections of your personality disordered parent. However, by unintentionally allowing this evolutionary pull, you are re-engaging in the traumatic material from your toxic parental exposure and re-experiencing various forms of trauma—again and again.

The practice of gratitude is designed to realign your focus with your positive experiences. It promotes a realistic balance in your emotional memory system—a balance that is healthy and necessary. Also, the ongoing practice of gratitude will help you to *maintain* this positive state of mind even when you aren't consciously focusing on it.

Responding, Not Reacting

In many dysfunctional families, emotions run high. These intense emotions are seemingly fueled by misperceptions around who is doing what to whom. Stated another way, these charged up emotions are oftentimes entangled in a great deal of personalization (i.e., "You did this to purposefully hurt me"), projection (i.e., ascribing one's own feelings, usually negative, to another), and negative attribution (i.e., accusatory explanations of cause). This complex emotional stew is further inflamed by the presence of alcohol and drugs, boundary violations, and emotional volatility. So, all in all, the dysfunctional family is ripe terrain for reacting.

In addition to the family dysfunctions that promote reacting, society unintentionally reinforces this tendency. There is the ingrained assumption that drama will get you attention and lead you to your anticipated goal or desired outcome. For example, television reality shows are typically all about drama. Also, this reactive dynamic of drama frequently plays out in the offices of lawyers and in courtrooms. Victims attempt to emotionally magnify their injuries while their lawyers enthusiastically exaggerate the damage done. All of this emotional intensity fuels a narcissistic drama that is based on *Me*.

Consider the following example we were told about. A patient spontaneously presented for a flu shot in a primary care office—without an appointment. The receptionist informed him that she would need to schedule him for an appointment later in the day or have him wait in the waiting room, which was full of ill patients, to be worked into the schedule. In other words, the non-emergent nature of his medical needs did not legitimize an unscheduled appointment.

The patient promptly became irate, screamed and yelled in front of the other patients, portrayed himself as a victim of the system, and then petulantly demanded to immediately see the office manager to complain. In response, the office manager accommodated him by having the staff work him quickly into the schedule, ahead of the other scheduled patients. This resulted in an unfair delay in the care of other patients that day as well as an unnecessary additional burden for the physician and staff members. After receiving his flu shot, the man briefly returned to the front desk to check out. He smirked and smugly told the receptionist, "See, I told you that I would get my flu shot today," as he tossed his billing slip towards her.

The preceding example illustrates reactionary and manipulative behavior. This kind of inappropriate behavior is typically coupled with a sense of injustice and entitlement. Reactionary behavior is experienced by the rest of us as manipulative and interpersonally offensive. From a psychological perspective, it's truly emotionally dishonest behavior coupled with bullying. It is all about Me and My needs. It's self-centered and unfortunately characteristic of individuals with personality disorders.

From a spiritual perspective, the thrust of personal growth is towards increasing emotional neutrality, rather than emotional reactivity. The aim or purpose of emotional neutrality is grounded on a number of spiritual principles. First and foremost, in terms of our fellow humans, emotional dumping and other manipulative behaviors are not appropriate—they purposefully and intentionally distress other people. These fellow humans are to be valued and respected by us as other spiritual entities. In the preceding example, this man obviously didn't care who he distressed (e.g., the receptionist, the other patients, the office manager, the physician) as long as *his* needs were met.

Whatever the momentary conflict or issue, it really isn't likely to be that important in the broader scheme of things or in the unending expanse of the life experience. Most daily conflicts and issues are typically minor, momentary, and based upon a Me-and-My-needs focus. "Someone stole my morning newspaper from the driveway." "They didn't call me back." "Here's a second notice, and I already paid that bill." In realistic terms, these issues are relatively unimportant. They are hardly worth igniting a toxic emotional eruption or undergoing a smoldering meltdown for the day. These reactions, not the incidents themselves, sacrifice one's well-being. These incidents shouldn't hold a life-or-death level of priority—they aren't leopards prowling through the savannah looking for a meal.

Reactionary behavior challenges another basic spiritual principle—accepting life's obstacles as opportunities for growth. Reacting entails complaining, distorting, grumbling, and manipulating others in an effort to avoid some obstacle. But remember, life's obstacles are *your* opportunities for growth. They are *your* paths in life. They are *not* intended as opportunities to emotionally dump onto others because of your unwillingness to deal with the life tasks at hand. In the preceding example, this self-centered patient could have easily anticipated his need for a flu shot, called the clinic, and scheduled an appointment—like the other patients being seen that day had done.

While much of this reactivity operates at a self-centered level, realize that society colors and distorts our view of obstacles, as well. A good life (or at least a lucky one) is supposed to be conflict-free. A successful life is free of problems. The existence of problems means something is wrong. In contrast to these Western assumptions, Eastern philosophy characterizes problems as ubiquitous and an inherent aspect of life. Problems exist to enrich our unique paths for growth. So, the society we are immersed in may influence how we view the inevitable—problems and obstacles—and our emotional reactions to them.

Finally, keep in mind that reactionary behavior tends to be a surface emotional response. It generally lacks any meaningful connection with one's deeper spiritual nature or core. Reactionary behavior is like a superficial ripple on the surface of the water. The deeper genuine emotional processes are like the depths of the ocean, lying far beneath the surface waves. Yes, there are times when momentary events are truly distressing. But begin to recognize that our deeper essence is more important and that most of our reactionary responses relate to minimally relevant issues. How important or relevant will these issues be tomorrow, next week, or next year? Yet, the harmful emotional charge of these destructive experiences continually adds to the negative emotional charge within us and on the planet generally, and tends to create an overall disharmonious atmosphere for other people.

In dealing with your personality disordered parent, we encourage you to continually assess your emotional reactivity. Use your emotional reactivity to gauge your own psychological and spiritual progress or growth. As you achieve greater mastery over the parental obstacle, you should notice a corresponding and increasing level of emotional neutrality. In other words, as you gain a greater and broader understanding of your parental situation and its meaning, you should also achieve a corresponding decrease in your emotional reactivity to situations. Respond rather than react.

Compassion

Compassion is a pervasive spiritual principle that encompasses the themes of empathy, genuine concern, kindness, and consideration towards others. Compassion is an outward focus, as opposed to an inward focus. It is a focus on *Them*, not *Me*. In this regard, compassion can functionally take you away from self-absorption and preoccupation with your own inner experiences to the emotional needs and experiences of another person. This inner-to-other shift in experience leaves you feeling better than continuing to focus on your own hurts.

Through exposure to the distress of others and the experience of compassion, we have the opportunity to truly connect with the deeper emotions and complex experiences of other individuals, which in turn, broadens our life knowledge and experience. We can easily appreciate the smallness of *Me* and the bigness of *Them*. We believe that this is a more realistic perspective in life—that life is bigger than all of us, and that we each are comparatively a miniscule molecule in an unending universe. We are interconnected and contribute to life as we humans know it, but we are also part of a far larger experience—one that cannot be imagined. Such a perspective wrenches us out of the entrenched narcissistic position of *Me*.

How do you cultivate compassion? It starts with empathy. Practice pausing with the feelings and emotions of others, and allow yourself to truly experience them. Compassion is an active experience and involves an immediate sense of feeling. It's important not to unintentionally side-step these emotional experiences by assuming that you've been compassionate by donating used clothes to the local thrift shop, tithing to your church, or giving a dollar to a beggar. While these are valued contributions in their own right, compassion involves the genuine emotional experiencing of another person and *that person's* experience. Allow it to pull you out of your own immediate experience, at least for the moment, and enable you to gain a broader knowledge of life.

How does this relate to personality disordered parents? We would encourage you to have compassion for their life situation. Most likely, they were the victims of complex and destructive dynamics that resulted in the warping of their personalities. As victims, they didn't really have a choice or a voice in the process. It just unfolded as it was. We believe that a necessary part of healing from your experiences with the personality disordered parent is to allow for a compassionate view of *their* circumstances. We are not saying, "They did the best they could." Most of the time, they probably could have done better. But, they were given liabilities, too, and we believe that these liabilities need to be recognized and acknowledged. As an example, recall that Romey had a number of undeniable liabilities, which deeply affected her throughout her entire lifetime. From a realistic perspective, she also made number of bad choices, as well. But, these bad choices did not undo the profound experience of abandonment and rejection that Romey endured during her life.

Surrender

Whenever we think about surrender, we frequently imagine the Wicked Witch of the West in the movie *The Wizard of Oz*, flying across the sky on her broomstick, writing out the words, "Surrender Dorothy" in dark smoke. Given this dramatic cinematic image, surrender is another word that has distinctly different Western and Eastern connotations. From a Western perspective, surrender implies giving up, giving in, and admitting defeat. From this vantage point, surrender maintains a very negative connotation.

From an Eastern perspective, surrender entails the concepts of acceptance, recognition, understanding, and acknowledgement. It is a position of allowing. In the context of a personality disordered parent, surrender means accepting your parental situation as it is or was. It means adopting the attitude that life unfolds as it is, and this includes your life, as well. Accept it as it is. It is what it is. In this way, the parental experience becomes more neutral and less emotion-laden.

As an example, during one particularly emotional session, a patient was acknowledging the many difficulties in her life. She seemed to genuinely accept these adversities, but was frustrated that her parents couldn't accept them. She proclaimed, "My life is what it is. This is *my* life. It's not their life. It's *my* life and it *is* what it *is*." She wasn't complaining. She was simply acknowledging her situation in a factual and non-judgmental manner.

The position of surrender also eliminates the "what-ifs." "What if I had a better parent? What if I had a more loving mother? What if I had a father who wasn't addicted to alcohol?" The reality is . . . you didn't. While these alternatives are certainly appealing, they are not real. They didn't happen and they won't happen. What-ifs are fantasies. In this respect, it's time for you to relinquish your fantasies. It is time to surrender, accept what happened, and make peace with your situation.

Before we leave this principle, we want to stress that surrender is *not* resignation or helplessness. Resignation does not involve genuine acceptance. Resignation is emotional refusal and passive tolerance of the situation. It is not a truly favorable reception to an idea or an experience. One of us recently spoke with a man in a wheelchair and inquired about his experience. He candidly admitted that life was more difficult in a wheelchair, but through the wheelchair, he had experienced life in deeper and more meaningful ways. He had surrendered to his situation in the service of learning and experiencing, regardless of the circumstances being less than ideal.

Forgiveness

We saved this spiritual principle for last because we believe that the principle of forgiveness is the most challenging one. What exactly is forgiveness? Quite frankly, it's a difficult principle to put into words. Forgiveness in a traditional sense means to absolve, excuse, pardon, or exonerate another of blame. Right at the outset, this concept gets a bit murky. To pardon or to excuse appears to imply that the infraction was not really that bad, is acceptable on some level, or is excusable. We do not want these associated beliefs to conflict with our impression of forgiveness, here. From a psychological perspective, we mean perhaps the best that we can achieve is an emotionally neutral stance and acceptance (not permission) of the infraction.

If you are able to neutrally accept the adversity that has happened to you, and to neutralize your emotions about it (dull down the anger and hurt), perhaps this is the truest form of forgiveness. Neutral acceptance without raw reactivity seems like a worthy (healthy) goal.

Some believe that it is easier to forgive if there is a clear causal explanation. "He or she did that because ..." For example, one individual might be able to more easily absolve another if the cause of the infraction were related to mental dysfunction. Suppose a man with undiagnosed bipolar disorder spent his entire life savings during a manic high, leaving his family in a very difficult spot financially. This devastating behavior can be reasonably rationalized by some and excused because the man suffers from an illness characterized by extreme hedonistic impulsivity, such as reckless spending. We could easily stretch this line of thinking to personality disordered parents. They, too, suffer from a bona fide psychiatric disorder. So, this same line of reasoning might be used to achieve a state of forgiveness (i.e., emotional neutrality) with regard to the personality disordered parent.

Importantly, forgiveness is not saying that the infraction was okay or acceptable. It is not saying that the perpetrator is free of responsibility. It is a means of disentangling emotionally from a negative situation with a perpetrator so as not to remain enmeshed and victimized by a past situation.

We encourage you to struggle with this principle, and to return to it repeatedly. Come to your own conclusions about it. We believe that this struggle is a necessary spiritual process and a *necessary* life experience. Remember that few things in life are black-and-white, cut-and-dried. Most things exist in the gray zone—the messy zone. And sometimes, spiritual growth, too, is messy.

Chapter 11
Embracing the Path

It is good to have an end to journey toward;
but it is the journey that matters, in the end.
Ursula K. Le Guin

At the start, we emphasized that we view the process described in this book as a journey. Now we want to qualify this concept by adding, " . . . without a beginning or an end." We believe that the journey of inner self-discovery—psychological and spiritual growth—is the greatest journey that we humans will undertake as individuals. This journey takes a great deal of courage and fortitude, yet is likely to be the most satisfying experience we will have. For this reason, we would like to frame the material in this book as simply a part of your unique and ongoing individual journey, a journey without a beginning or an end.

Note that a key portion of this journey entails the rethinking of obstacles. In this regard, there is a potential greater good in having personality disordered parents. Through transcending these challenging and disruptive parents (obstacles), you have the potential to experience a unique type of growth that simply cannot be achieved in any other way. Unfortunately, the challenge of personality disordered parents can understandably serve as a justification for failed relationships, depression, low self-esteem, addictions, and various other forms of self-destructive behavior—all unhealthy detours from the path. Or, the experiences from having a personality disordered parent can be incorporated into the context of your life's purpose.

From a spiritual perspective, surely personality disordered parents have to serve some greater purpose for their offspring. Perhaps that greater purpose is to powerfully motivate their children to grow, thereby enabling a degree of forward momentum that might not be possible with a childhood of contentment. As such, these disordered parents may be truly unique opportunities.

As you move forward, an ongoing challenge may be keeping the material in this book from fading into the background of your conscious awareness. Of course that is indeed the long-term goal—to resolve issues so that you are literally beyond experiencing them negatively. However, to get there requires psychological and spiritual effort because the temptation is always to go back to old habits and ways of thinking and feeling. These old ways may not be satisfying, but they represent the known and predictable path. It can be difficult to keep from slipping back into the worn grooves of the old path, and recognizing when that is indeed what has happened.

The challenge is to nourish the principles that you have learned into an active, ongoing, and living *experience*. Harness these principles and incorporate them into your daily life. Rather than "working through" the material, as if it had a beginning and an end, use it as a set of dynamic principles for your ongoing life experience. Come back to them again and again.

Along any journey, we sometimes need to stop and ask for assistance. Perhaps there seems to be something blocking us from further growth, but we can't even see what that might be. Or perhaps we see it, but don't know how to use it for our growth (rather than only seeing it as an obstacle). If you believe that you need additional assistance, we encourage you to consult with a therapist, counselor, or spiritual advisor in an effort to enhance your own growth.

We close this book by sincerely wishing you well on your personal journey. Because you are reading this book, we know that your journey most likely has been a painful and challenging one. We know that you have struggled. We know that you have been hurt. We know that you have suffered. We also know that you are a seeker, or you would never have picked up this book. We know you are motivated to grow—to experience life differently. Don't stop seeking. Continue to experience. Continue to learn. Continue to embrace your path.

About the Authors

Randy A. Sansone, M.D., is a professor of psychiatry and internal medicine at Wright State University School of Medicine in Dayton, OH. Dr. Sansone has published more than 400 articles and book chapters. He co-edited the books *Self-Harm Behavior and Eating Disorders* and *Personality Disorders and Eating Disorders*, and co-authored the book *Borderline Personality Disorder in the Medical Setting*. Dr. Sansone has maintained an active interest in the treatment and research of personality disorders throughout his career.

Michael W. Wiederman, Ph.D., is a professor of psychology at Columbia College in Columbia, SC. Dr. Wiederman has published more than 200 articles. He authored the book *Understanding Sexuality Research* and co-edited the *Handbook for Conducting Research on Human Sexuality*.

17067235R00121

Made in the USA
Charleston, SC
25 January 2013